FROM BIRDIES
TO BUNKERS

From Birdies to Bunkers

Discover How Golf Can Bring
Love, Humor, and Success
Into Your Life

ALICE DYE

WITH MARK SHAW

HarperResource
An Imprint of *HarperCollins*Publishers

HarperCollins books may be purchased for educational, business, or sales promotional use. For information please write: Special Markets Department, HarperCollins Publishers Inc., 10 East 53rd Street, New York, NY 10022.

Photograph on page 27 © AP/Wide World Photos
Photograph on page 60 © *The Herald Weekly* Photographic Collection

FIRST EDITION
Designed by Nicola Ferguson

Library of Congress Cataloging-in-Publication Data

Dye, Alice.
From birdies to bunkers : discover how golf can bring love, humor, and success into your life / Alice Dye with Mark Shaw.—1st ed.
p.   cm.
Includes index.
ISBN 0-06-052821-4
1. Dye, Alice.   2. Women golfers—United States—Biography.
3. Golf course architects—United States—Biography.   4. Golfers—Conduct of life.   I. Shaw, Mark, 1945–   II. Title.

GV964.D94A34   2004
796.352'092—dc22
[B]   2003056658

04 05 06 07 08 WBC/QW 10 9 8 7 6 5 4 3 2 1

Dedicated to:

PETE DYE

MY HUSBAND, MY PARTNER, MY CHAMPION

When you hit a poor shot, get over it fast and start thinking about the next shot and how you are going to hit a great recovery. Do not dwell on a miss-hit, but love the challenge of the next shot. Stay positive. Just how poorly would you have to play to wish you were back at the office working or home housecleaning?

ALICE DYE GOLF ACHIEVEMENTS

COMPETITIONS

CHAMPION, USGA Senior Women's Amateur, 1978–79

RUNNER-UP, USGA Senior Women's Amateur, 1977, 1981, 1989

CHAMPION, North and South Amateur

CHAMPION, Women's Eastern Amateur

CHAMPION, Doherty-Jones

THREE-TIME CHAMPION, Florida State Women's Amateur

NINE-TIME CHAMPION, Indiana State Women's Amateur

ELEVEN-TIME CHAMPION, Indianapolis Metropolitan Championship

TWELVE-TIME QUALIFIER, USGA Women's Open

SEMIFINALIST, USGA Women's Amateur

WOMEN'S CLUB CHAMPION, Seminole, Crooked Stick, Gulfstream Golf Club, Woodstock Country Club

MEMBER, 1970 United States Curtis Cup Team

CHAMPION, National Club Championship for Women
CHAMPION, Senior Olympic Golf

HONORS
Indiana State Golf Hall of Fame
CAPTAIN, USGA Women's World Cup Team
USGA Isaac Grainger Award for Dedicated Service
Spirit of Golf Award
Don Rossi Award for Lifetime Contribution to Golf
Indiana Heritage Outstanding Achievement Award
Red Coat Award for Celebrity of the Year
Women's Western Golf Association Woman of
     Distinction Award
Lily of France Award for Outstanding Achievement
First Florida's Outstanding Achievement Award
Youthlinks Indiana Pathfinder Award

SERVICE
FIRST WOMAN MEMBER, Board of Directors, PGA of
     America
FIRST WOMAN MEMBER, American Society of Golf
     Course Architects
FIRST WOMAN PRESIDENT, American Society of Golf
     Course Architects
BOARD MEMBER, Women's Western Golf Association
STEERING COMMITTEE, 20/20
USGA Women's Executive Committee

USGA Women's Handicap Committee
LPGA Advisory Committee
First Tee Advisory Committee

NOTABLE PETE AND ALICE DYE GOLF COURSES

Austin Country Club, TX
Avalon Lakes, OH
*Blackwolf Run, WI
Brickyard Crossing, IN
Bridgewater, IN
*Bulle Rock, MD
Carmel Valley Ranch Golf Club, CA
Colleton River—Dye Course, SC
*Crooked Stick Golf Club, IN
*Disney World—Cypress Course, FL
Dye Fore, Dominican Republic
Dye Preserve, FL
Firethorn Golf Club, NE
*Harbour Town Golf Links, SC
Kingsmill—River Course, VA
*La Romana Country Club, Dominican Republic
Long Cove Club, SC
Mission Hills—Dye Course, CA
Mystic Rock at Nemacolin, PA
*Oak Tree, OK
*Old Marsh Golf Club, FL

Paiute—Las Vegas, NV

Radrick Farms Golf Club, MI

Stonebridge Country Club, TX

*Teeth of the Dog, Dominican Republic

The Citrus Course at La Quinta, CA

The Dye Course—PGA Village, FL

*The Golf Club, OH

*The Honors, TN

The Kampen Course at Purdue, IN

*The Medalist Course with Greg Norman, FL

*The Mountain Course at La Quinta, CA

*The Ocean Course at Kiawah, SC

*The Pete Dye Club, WV

*The Stadium Course at PGA West, CA

*The Tournament Players Course at Sawgrass, FL

*Whistling Straits and The Irish, WI

*Listed in *Golf Magazine*'s Top 100 Courses

CONTENTS

FOREWORD

When Alice Dye asked me to write the foreword to *From Birdies to Bunkers*, I was honored. Throughout my life, special people have influenced me and been an inspiration. Alice is certainly one of them.

I first met Alice as a teenager learning how to play competitive golf. My parents encouraged me to compete in as many tournaments as possible, and one of them was the Women's Western Amateur. I was only fourteen, but my skills had improved to the point where I was a contender. Some of the older players were threatened by my ability, but Alice was not. From our first meeting, she was friendly and considerate. I realized right away that she was the type of player, and the type of woman, I wanted to be. She encouraged me, and this meant a great deal to someone who wasn't being treated very well by other players.

I recall my parents commenting on how Alice treated me. She was so nice; she wanted to help, to provide me with words of wisdom furthering both my maturity as a youngster and my golf skills. When we met in a match, it didn't matter that I was three decades younger; she treated me as an equal. After I was fortunate enough to beat her, she smiled, shook my hand, and wished me well. What a class act, I thought to myself.

I can remember Alice's long, comfortable, smooth golf swing like it was yesterday. She was a confident, aggressive, ranked player, the type I knew I would have to beat to have a chance of winning a tournament. Amateur golf was a great time in my life. I loved the fellowship and the competitiveness. Playing women like Alice toughened my resolve and showed me how good I needed to be to succeed.

Besides her fluid golf swing, what impressed me about Alice was her demeanor. She was a dogged competitor, determined and focused, never afraid to attempt a great shot. All I wanted to do at the time was get the ball in the hole a little bit faster than my opponent, but when you played Alice, you'd better be ready to take chances. Match play was a great training ground because you risked hitting tough shots, knowing that if you failed, you only lost the one hole. This is what made it exciting. Alice and others like her could hit those great shots, intimidating other players. I watched how she played, how she planned her shots, how she had a strategy in mind. I saw a competitor I wanted to be like, and I never forgot the lessons learned from this great lady.

Perhaps the most important thing I noted about Alice was her way of handling winning and losing. She taught me a lot about how not to pout when I lost and not to be arrogant when I won. I've played with so many players who never learned this, but I'm thankful I had Alice and others like her as role models. She has as much drive and determination as any woman I have ever met, but she is a gracious lady, respected by all in the game. Alice competed, and if she won, she was thrilled. If she lost, she did not make excuses or attempt to belittle her opponent. As long as she knew she had tried her best, she accepted defeat and tried to get better.

Another trait Alice possesses is that she is never inclined to talk about how good she is. This is a common thread among the great players, and she is certainly one of the greatest amateur golfers who ever lived. But if you talk to her, you'd never know it. You always sense her abilities when you are with her or competing against her, but she lets her golf do the talking. She's a down-to-earth person despite her worthy accomplishments, ones that include championships around the country won during six decades.

Alice Dye's selection to the prestigious Curtis Cup while she was in her forties is amazing. I'm surprised she was never selected before, but can you imagine the determination it takes to compete for so many years before becoming a Curtis Cup team member? I know how much it meant to me to be selected and play; I can only imagine how she felt when the Stars and Stripes were raised on the first tee.

Alice is one of the most positive individuals I have ever met. When you are around her, she radiates "can-do." My friends and colleagues in the golf world know that if she is on the committee or lends her name to a cause or an issue in any way, sparks will fly and things will get done. This is why she is so respected by everyone in golf who knows her. If Alice says she will do something, you can count on it.

Through the years as a female architect, Alice has been a crusader for improving the playability of the game for women. Whether as a partner with her husband, Pete, or as a member of numerous golf committees, she has worked hard to make certain that the women's viewpoint is considered. When I designed the Villages Golf Course in Ocala, Florida, many of my ideas regarding alternative tees were influenced by Alice. Golfers should be able to choose how much pressure they want to endure with a shot, and like her, I want the challenge to be fair. When it is, the player is rewarded for a good shot but not severely penalized for an errant one.

Speaking of Pete, I once told him after playing the Blackwolf Run, his course in Kohler, Wisconsin, "I don't like you very much." Thank God Alice has been alongside to temper some of his "interesting" ideas for courses, since she knows the importance of the playability factor. Alice tells a wonderful story in this book about her influence on the famous island-green hole at the TPC in Florida. I laugh every time I read it.

Above all, Alice Dye loves golf, and her love for the game is infectious. In this book, she recounts many of the special moments in her life and includes thoughts about playing the game that will benefit everyone. Whether she's telling the story of her first set of clubs, competing with "the Babe," learning the game from Tommy Armour, matching strokes with "Big Mama," partnering with Pete at the Harbour Town Golf Links, or providing a strong opinion about golf ball and club technology, *From Birdies to Bunkers* blends real information with humor and is guaranteed to entertain readers.

I hope many parents with kids who are interested in the game will make this book required reading, since the lessons learned from Alice provide guideposts both for golf and for living. I am fortunate to have known this unforgettable woman, and I'm flattered to call her my friend.

—*Nancy Lopez*

INTRODUCTION

Golf champion, respected golf course architect, women's golf pioneer, mentor, friend—that, and more, is Alice O'Neal Dye. From making birdies to defeat opponents in major amateur championships to building bunkers with her husband, Pete, creating many of the greatest golf courses in America, Alice is a true renaissance woman.

For starters, Alice is one of the greatest women amateur golfers ever to take club to ball. She won her first championship at age fourteen and is still winning championships in her seventh decade. At age seventy-four, she captured the Crooked Stick Golf Club Women's Club Championship in hundred-degree heat.

Alice's golf competition achievements are listed on the opening pages of this book. She has been beating opponents who underestimated her ability ever since she was a cute, leggy teenager with the concentration of a seasoned professional. Through the years, Alice has collected championship trophies that could fill a warehouse. When she tackled the lady professionals, Alice finished third in an LPGA event behind Hall of Famers Mickey Wright and Kathy Whitworth. In 1966 *Golf Digest* listed Alice as the second-ranked woman amateur in the world, behind French champion Caterine LaCoste.

Alice has competed in the USGA Women's Senior Amateur *twenty-four* times and counting. Twice she won; three times she finished runner-up. In the 1970 Curtis Cup matches Alice played the pivotal match. When the captain told her the team was in trouble, she came through by winning the final three holes. This mindset was epitomized by the answer I received when I asked Pete whether it was important to Alice that she win a member/guest tournament at the fabled Seminole Golf Club in Florida. "Some people at seventy-five years old would be happy they can walk," he said with a twinkle in his eye. "Alice is not. She wants to win." This attitude caused the immortal Chick Evans to write of Alice, "She's a lady golfer with a fighting heart."

In 1958 Pete and Alice were reigning Indiana State Amateur champions. Reporter William Fox wrote, "Mr. and Mrs. Pete Dye had better watch it. Otherwise, they might find themselves being prosecuted under Federal monopoly laws." In a later article, Fox called Alice "The Queen of Short Irons."

If Alice, an intimidating player known for her competitive spirit, is well known as a champion of champions among women's amateur golfers, she is even more respected as a woman of vision in an arena dominated by men. A gifted golf course architect determined to give back to the game she loves, Alice, without a plan or an agenda, became a pioneer, a woman of firsts. Never one to believe that a woman should be deterred from seeking any goal, she was honored to be the first woman elected as president of the American Society of Golf Course Architects. A few years later, she achieved another woman of firsts honor when the PGA of America, the governing body for the thousands of club professionals, appointed Alice to their Board of Directors. CEO Jim Awtrey said of her term, "Alice's contributions were significant. Thank God for Alice." The contributions he referred to included Alice's emphasis on the use of unisex language in PGA directives to their woman members. "Business attire" replaced "coat and tie," and "spouse" replaced "wife." Alice also was an advocate of adjusted yardages in PGA of America tournaments so that men and women professionals could compete fairly. This change directly influenced the ability of Susan Whatley to qualify for and compete in a PGA Tour event in 2003.

A major contribution of Alice and Pete is the evolution of the Golf for Business and Life Collegiate Program, a part of the PGA's Growth of the Game program. Jim Awtrey would be interested to learn that the lovely plaque awarded to Alice for service to the PGA is leaning against other memorabilia on the floor in the small office the Dyes keep in their Delray Beach, Florida, home. Alice is proud of the plaque—she just doesn't flaunt her achievements.

Alice the innovator has surfaced, no matter what golf organization she has served. A fifty-year member of the Women's Western Golf Association board, she secured new tournament sites and has assisted with course setup and rules. The Women's Western honored her with their Woman of Distinction Award and named their senior championship trophy the Alice O'Neal Dye Award.

When Alice became president of the American Society of Golf Course Architects, she worked to upgrade the professional aspects of the group. She established the Paul Fullmer Trophy, to be awarded to the winner of the annual associate member golf tournament. The trophy, featuring a pipe on top, was so beloved that Fullmer refused to allow the winner to take it home.

Membership in the society symbolized Alice's respect among her peers. When she submitted her application, Fullmer said, there was discussion as to whether a woman should become a member. Dick Nugent, a former football player and wrestler, told Paul he had some apprehensions. Checking Alice's credentials, Nugent telephoned Joe Webster, the owner of a course being constructed in Florida where Alice was working with Pete. Dick said to

Joe, "What would happen if Pete croaked while the course was being built?" Joe replied, "Alice would finish it better, faster, and cheaper." Nugent then called Fullmer and said, "Alice has my vote."

At age twenty-seven, as the youngest-ever member of the USGA Women's Executive Committee, Alice was instrumental in convincing the USGA to provide uniforms for members of the Curtis Cup and World teams. She also championed the selection of a former member of the team to be chosen as a captain. While a member of the USGA handicap committee, Alice advocated "real world" handicapping concepts instead of those based on theory, providing a much more practical means to handicap players.

In May 2002, Rollins College, Alice's alma mater, presented her with an honorary doctorate in humanities. When Alice told me the news, I overheard Pete, who had never graduated from grade school, high school, or college, say, "I got mine first," referring to Purdue University awarding him an honorary doctorate in 1999.

When controversy surrounded Augusta National Golf Club, home of the famed Masters, regarding the absence of a woman member, *GolfWeek* magazine handicapped women who could be considered "candidates" for membership. They included Alice's name. She was listed at 25–1 odds, below Nancy Lopez, Judy Bell, and Peggy Kirk Bell but ahead of Supreme Court Justice Sandra

Day O'Connor. When I asked Alice about the mention, she was unimpressed.

Alice's contributions to women's golf are without precedent. With bulldog persistence, she has convinced golf course designers to assess how the game can be more enjoyable for women. Her innovative thoughts spearheaded the drive to provide forward tees. Previously they were called ladies' tees—nothing more than markers positioned just a few yards in front of the men's tees. Journalist Hal Phillips dubbed Alice "The patron saint of forward tees." The title is appropriate. Every woman golfer owes Alice a debt of gratitude for her steadfast effort to ensure that the game is fair, manageable, and more enjoyable.

Alice's focus on playability, Pete's creativity—a perfect team, one that began when Pete spotted Alice, whom he called "Legs," at Rollins College in Orlando. The two exchanged vows on Groundhog Day, 1950. It is a wonderful love story, filled with respect and caring. When Pete awakens in the morning, there is "Ally," as he calls her, holding a cup of coffee, a banana, and the morning newspaper. If you want to see true love in action, just watch the way the Dyes look at each other.

Pete and Alice treat each other as equals. There is no jealousy regarding individual accomplishments. They are willing to assist each other in any pursuit, always finding time to do so. Both are golf course designers and past presidents of the American Society of Golf Course Architects. Each has been recognized with an honorary college doctorate. Both have won state amateur golf championships and served on a Western Golf Association board. Both were captains of their college golf teams and later members of the Indiana Golf Hall of Fame. Each has now written a book.

Pete and Alice Dye golf courses are listed at the beginning of this book—such golf jewels as Whistling Straits, Herb Kohler's gem in Wisconsin, site of the 2004 PGA Championship; Harbour Town Golf Links; the Ocean Course at Kiawah, site of the memorable 1991 Ryder Cup Matches; Crooked Stick, site of John Daly's victory in the PGA Championship; the Honors Golf Club, Jack Lupton's venue for amateur championships; and the heaven-sent Teeth of the Dog in the Dominican Republic, where seven holes border the crystal blue Caribbean. More Dye courses open every year.

Alice resisted my request to write this book. I was privileged to assist Pete with his autobiography, *Bury Me in a Pot Bunker,* but Alice was not interested in telling her story. For years, yes, *years,* I continued to encourage her, believing that the story was worthy; that it must be told. Watching Alice when she played, worked with Pete, mentored young people, and cast her wisdom among so many made me realize there were many lessons, about golf as well as life, that could be learned from her.

I became aware of the Alice "golf mentality," as I dub it, the first time I ever met her. In the late 1960s a mutual friend, Wayne Timberman Jr., invited me to play golf with the Dyes at Crooked Stick. When I approached the first tee, I shook hands with a wiry fellow in khaki shorts and a porkpie hat and a woman twenty years my senior with a ready smile. A dollar bet for nine holes was suggested. I quickly accepted, realizing that if I couldn't beat Pete Dye, I certainly could beat "the lady in the group."

The match between me—a former member of the Purdue University Golf Team—and "the lady in the group" was over before it began. Alice hit her drive down the middle of the fairway, then holed the second shot for an eagle two. She won nine holes; I won none. Dollar lost and paid. Welcome to the world of Alice Dye, one of the most dogged competitors ever to play golf.

When Alice finally agreed to record her golf memories, I traveled to the Dye home in Delray Beach, Florida. Sixty, a black German shepherd, greeted me. She is Pete's pal and a famous jet dog, traveling on the seats of the aircraft transporting Pete from course to course. Sixty may be disappointed when she visits dog heaven, since her life in the hereafter cannot possibly match her life on this earth. The Dye's friend Wayne Timberman says Sixty hit the dog lottery.

Working with Alice was a challenge, since she is one of

those let-my-work-speak-for-itself types. As we scanned scrapbooks filled with memories, discussed the different aspects of her long and successful career, and noted people whom she respected, I realized that as Alice spoke, her words of wisdom transcended the game of golf. I encouraged Alice to broaden the scope of the book to include life skills that had permitted her to be successful in so many different arenas. I felt that she could inspire and influence men and women of all ages, whether they were golfers or not.

As Alice's stories evolved, I was fascinated with the lessons-learned aspect of her life. Some of Alice's words reflected on how the game of golf is played and the strategies to be employed. Others defined her wonderful sense of humor, revealing personal moments that caused me to laugh. When you read the pigeon story, you will understand why. Like others the Dyes have adopted, the pigeon enjoyed several months of loving care before flying off to who knows where.

During my visit, Alice's brother, Perry O'Neal, USGA Senior Women's Amateur champion Carol Semple Thompson, and Pete Dye provided additional glimpses into Alice's world. Diane Darsch chipped in with a memorable quote: "Above all, Alice cares. She loves life, and she loves people. When you enter Alice's life, she adopts you."

Diane is correct; love for others is the Alice Dye staple. So enjoy the essays from this pioneering woman of firsts, whose belief in herself, dedication, and hard work provide inspiration to anyone she meets. Alice Dye has been a winner all her life; here's just part of the story.

—*Mark Shaw*

From Horses to Courses

In 1927, when I was six months old, my mother held me in her arms as we gazed skyward to watch Charles Lindbergh fly over Indianapolis, Indiana. He had just returned from his historic thirty-three-and-a-half-hour solo flight over the Atlantic Ocean from New York to Paris. This same year, my grandfather Holliday purchased twenty-two acres from the north portion of land owned by the Crown Hill Cemetery. Grandfather, president of W. J. Holliday Steel Co., rerouted Forty-second Street to become the south boundary of his property. He named his new estate Shooters Hill, after his forefathers' place of origin outside of London, England.

Shooters Hill was bounded to the north by a steep ravine that bottomed to the canal and the White River. Butler University and the Shortridge High School football field were to the east, and the J. K. Lilly estate was to the west. My grandparents built their home, a teahouse, a caretaker's house, a barn, and a large vegetable garden on the western portion of the estate. A few years later my parents built our home on the eastern side, and my mother's brother, W. J. Holliday, built his home nearby.

My mother was an avid gardener. She surrounded our house with beautiful gardens and two greenhouses full of orchids. Her sport was fly-fishing, and she was quite an expert.

My father was a partner in the Thompson, O'Neal and Smith law firm. He loved golf. His baseball swing, descended from his college team sport, served him well at nearby Woodstock's nine-hole layout, built in 1916 by Tom Bendelow.

Country living was lonesome for a young girl. There were no neighborhood children to play with because of our rural location. In the winter months, school activities kept me busy. During the summer, the Woodstock Country Club, only a bike ride away, offered camp-style classes in swimming, diving, tennis, and golf. The club became the center of my social life. I formed friendships with other children my age; learned how to swim, dive, and play tennis; and was introduced to golf.

Golf professional George Stark ran the small wooden golf shop and caddie yard. The summer I was eleven, I joined his swing class, using a set of my mother's hickory-shafted clubs.

Mr. Stark taught the long, flowing arm swing popular with Scottish professionals. There were no practice ranges in those days, but there was not much play on weekday mornings. He instructed us as we hit balls across fairways between the few groups of players. I loved hitting the balls and did not mind having to run out and pick them all up. Without much more direction, we were sent out to play on the course.

After playing a few holes, the other kids went back to the swimming pool and tennis courts, but I went on alone. I loved the feel of contact with the ball and the challenge of a good shot. While I enjoyed my school's sports and Woodstock's swim team and tennis games, the individual aspect of golf intrigued me. It was just me, the club, the ball, the joy of hitting a good shot, and, eventually, the challenge of shooting a good score. My golf club became a wand that waved me into a successful future. What a gift to give a child!

Mother and most women of her generation considered golf a game for men. A few women played on weekday mornings, but the ladies' tee markers were only a few yards ahead of the men's, making for a discouragingly long course.

Horseback riding was considered a proper sport for ladies. From the first time my father took me to the riding stable at the Meridian Hills Country Club, I wanted a horse of my own. Nagging sometimes wins, and my parents eventually bought me a circus horse named Taffy. She knew how to gallop and hold her back steady so that a bareback circus rider could not fall. Neither could I.

Taffy was fun to ride, but her stable was miles from my home, and the swing class lessons at Woodstock had ignited a spark. With my wood-shafted clubs in a little light bag, I played alone on weekday mornings when the course was fairly deserted. I wanted to shoot a good score, so when I hit a poor shot, I dropped the bag, ran after the ball, brought it back, and tried again . . . and maybe again. Dropping a different ball was not an option; I figured that would not count. I usually managed a score of about 45, playing by my rules. Having to chase a miss-hit ball and bring it back to try again really taught me to concentrate on every shot. Concentration became the mainstay of my golf game for the rest of my life.

Wood to Steel

By the age of fourteen, I was in love with golf and devoted my summers to the game. I still played with my mother's old set of clubs, but I coveted a set of eight steel-shafted clubs displayed in the Woodstock Club golf shop. There was a driver; a fairway wood; three-, five-, seven-, eight-, and nine-irons; and a sand wedge—all with glistening steel shafts. I wanted to ask my parents to buy them, but they were away on an extended fishing trip in the wilds of Canada. Calling them was not an option.

Determined to convince my parents that the new set was needed, I wrote an eight-page letter—one page for each treasured club, explaining exactly why I needed it to play Woodstock's nine holes. There were no faxes or Federal Express service in those days, so the letter was sent Air Mail Special Delivery, addressed to my father, since I knew he would be the most sympathetic.

Days passed as I anxiously awaited a response. Finally a telegram arrived. It read: "Buy them—they don't eat all winter," a reference to my horse, Taffy.

Armed with the new clubs, I began to score legitimately with no retakes . . . well, maybe a putt. My friends swam and played tennis, so I played alone or sometimes with one of the boys from the caddie shack. Only greens and tees were watered in those days, so by July the fairways became firm, and shots rolled wonderful distances. My new steel shafts did their job, my scores improved, and I finally broke 90. I was sad to see winter come but looked forward to the next spring.

In 1942 World War II was in its second year, but some golf organizations tried to continue to stage tournaments. Because of the wartime gasoline restrictions, the

Indiana State Girls Junior Championship was played as a two-day medal play event in three different cities. Woodstock's wartime golf professional, Wally Nelson, had been encouraging me and thought I was ready for the challenge, so he entered me in the tournament. I was now, at the age of fifteen, competing in my first official golf tournament.

No retakes of poor shots or missed putts were now permitted, but on the sixth tee I accidentally struck the ball with my practice swing, and it bounded into a bush. Scared to death, I asked my caddie, who was also my scorer, what to do. He was puzzled too but suggested I find the ball, re-tee, and continue playing. Worried, I played on. After completing the round, I was very relieved to learn that I would not be penalized because I was not intentionally trying to hit my drive. I posted an 88, and the next day's round of 92 was without incident. When the scores from the other cities were tallied, my total score was low by one shot. I was the Indiana State Girls Junior Champion. The prize was five dollars worth of war bond stamps, and my name was to be engraved on the large silver trophy. I was elated to win my first tournament.

I Can Do Anything Boys Can Do

There was no girl's golf team when I attended Short-ridge High School in Indianapolis. Few girls, if any, played, and it was even unfashionable for girls to go to gym class.

The first thing a girl requested when school began was a pass to skip gym. I often see women today trying to play golf who were "gym passers." They have a difficult time because they chose not to play sports in school. Every girl should have the opportunity and be encouraged to play some kind of team or individual sport. All this fun and experience should not be limited to boys. In addition, sports foster teamwork and build confidence and skills that enhance life.

Fortunately, before becoming a student at Short-ridge, I had attended Orchard School, a progressive grade school that encouraged students to participate in all sports. The teachers believed that boys and girls should have equal opportunities. Everyone went to shop and to weaving classes. Everyone was taught basketball, football, baseball—all the sports. The philosophy was that you could do anything. We were not segregated into "girls can do this," and "boys can do that," a principle that has stayed with me my entire life.

I never felt like I could not do something because I was a girl, but when I graduated from Orchard School and went to Shortridge High School, I succumbed to peer pressure and requested a gym pass. Winter weather prevented playing golf, but I missed sports and sneaked into the gym for the after-class basketball games. I certainly did not want my friends to know I was in gym-suit bloomers, running around the court. Shortridge presented the letter *S* to players making a team, and on awards day, in front of the whole school, I was called up onto the stage to receive my letter for basketball. It was one of the most embarrassing moments of my life.

Four years later at Rollins College, where there was a very positive attitude toward women in sports, I was proud to receive my letter *R* for basketball and golf.

Galleries

My father always encouraged me to work on my golf game. When I was fifteen years old, he surprised me by asking if I would like to play with his Saturday-afternoon foursome. He arranged for me to hit third—right in the middle of the group. I was very nervous but excited to show off my skills. After his first two gentlemen friends teed off, it was my turn to drive. My hand shook as I teed up the ball and tried a few practice swings. I managed only a feeble drive. I did not have far to walk to play my second shot, and I was determined to hit a good one. My father's foursome stood patiently nearby while I took a smooth practice swing. I addressed the ball and began my swing. Wanting to see how far my shot was going to travel, I took my eyes off the ball and whiffed. I was devastated.

My father gave me an affectionate and understanding smile, and I lasted a few more poorly played holes. I know he and his friends were proud of me for trying so hard, but it was my first experience with the pressure created by even a small friendly gallery. I was confused at the effect it had on my game.

My first encounter with a real gallery came the next year in the semifinal match of the Indianapolis City Championship. I was a leggy teenager playing a veteran. When I arrived at the first tee, I was horrified to see it surrounded by about fifty spectators. I did not whiff, but I did not get the ball airborne on my first drive . . . or any other shot for the first nine holes. Firm fairways and open green approaches saved me from a quick defeat, but nothing could save me from being completely mortified. Finally, on the back nine, my nerves settled a little as I began to take my mind off of the spectators and focus on my swing and making contact with the ball. My shots improved, and a little confidence crept back into my game. I even won a few holes, but I lost the match.

At some time, almost everyone experiences the pressure of being watched by others. It may be felt as you are teeing off before waiting foursomes, playing through a group, or being paired with a celebrity. This is not the time to try to improve your swing. Allow your mind to go back to the basics, focusing on rhythm, balance, and contact with the ball. Your body will relax and get back in the flow of your game.

Keeping Score

When I first began to keep an honest score, I used five as a base for each hole instead of par. Scoring even fives would result in a score of 45 for nine holes. As I improved, I would begin to figure my score under fives.

At age nineteen, I was playing a terrific round in the Indianapolis City Championship at the Country Club of Indianapolis. When I walked off the eighteenth green, sports reporter Bill Fox asked me, "How did you play?" Trying to figure out how many were under a five on each hole, I had almost lost count, but I said, "I think I am nineteen under." Bewildered, Mr. Fox took my card and tabulated a 71.

Years later, while attempting to qualify for the USGA Women's Amateur, I was struggling with my game. The night before, I had to attend a small beach party given by my hostess. Annoyed at having to socialize with strangers, I was trying to be pleasant to my dinner companion, who was pleased with her score that day in a local event. The lady told me she had shot a 78. I said that I sure wished I could shoot a 78 the next day. She said, "It's easy. All you need are two threes, two fours, and no sixes on each nine."

The idea worked, and I was the low qualifier. I learned two things: how to shoot 78 and that good ideas may come when you listen.

The Cottage

In 1911 my grandfather Holliday bought a cottage that was built in 1897 on the east side of Lake Maxinkuckee, home of Culver Military Academy, in northern Indiana.

As a child, my family brought my brother, Perry, and me there when we were not attending summer camps. We sailed, water-skied, swam, hunted turtles, and dug worms for fishing.

Right behind our cottage was the nine-hole Maxinkuckee Country Club, built by William Langford in 1922.

As I grew into my teenage years, I carried my little bag of clubs and played alone. Only the greens were watered, and by midsummer the ball rolled a long way on the fairways. Being able to hit my shots a long distance was encouraging. Even a missed shot would bounce along toward the target. My scores kept improving, and that inspired me to keep playing.

The Culver Military Academy was still all male, but it held dances every other Saturday night. We "lake girls" were invited, and since we were outnumbered by the cadets, it was not hard to be popular.

Many of us had our first kiss from a Culver cadet. I had a huge crush on one cadet who totally ignored me. His name was similar to Bobby Jones, and I had golf balls with the signature of Bobby Jones on them. I would position the ball so the name was facing me, and venting my frustration, I would hit that ball as hard as I could.

Years later, when Pete and I were young newlyweds, we hosted some rather wild house parties at the cottage that included trips to football games at Notre Dame thirty-five miles north in South Bend.

When our sons, Perry and P. B., were young, we took them to the cottage to swim, sail, catch fireflies, hunt turtles, and dig up worms—the same things I loved as a child. But even before they began their teenage years, both boys deserted the cottage and started working on Pete's construction jobs.

After they were married, both boys returned to the cottage, bringing friends and their children. Our grandchildren, Lucy and Lilly Dye, love the lake cottage just as I did. My brother, Perry O'Neal, lives in the cottage during the summer months and works hard to keep this hundred-year-old house in shape. Just as Pete and I keep the original concept of our golf courses but remodel them to keep up with the times, my brother and I have kept the concept of a summer lake house but installed modern conveniences such as a dishwasher, heat, and air-conditioning.

Pete and I have little time to visit our cottage, as summer construction jobs keep us busy. When we do go back, I still love to play the course, where I remember so many of the shots I hit as I was learning to play golf, especially the ones when I hit Bobby Jones's name on the golf ball because of the cadet who took no notice of me.

The Babe

In 1942, when I was fifteen, my mother asked my friend and good player, seventeen-year-old Carolyn Pickering (Lautner) to take me with her to the prestigious

Women's Western Amateur in Chicago. This organization tried to continue with their tournament in spite of the difficult wartime restrictions.

Driving to Chicago was impossible because of gas rationing, so Carolyn and I boarded the train and stayed in a downtown hotel. We had to take the El to the course and walk from the station carrying our clubs and shoes. For the first time, I saw the best women amateur players in the country compete. The tournament field included Dorothy Germain (Porter), Phyllis Otto (Germain), Betty Jameson, Dot Kirby, Polly Riley, and Ann Casey (Johnson).

The field did not include Patty Berg. Four years earlier, in 1938, she had won this tournament, plus the

Alice (left) with Lee Bongart (second from left), Peggy Kirk, and Dot Kirby.

USGA Women's Amateur, and played on the Curtis Cup team. Two years later, Patty turned professional to represent Wilson Sporting Goods Company. She then served as a lieutenant in the Marine Corps during World War II.

Mildred "Babe" Didrikson Zaharias won the 1940 Women's Western Open but did not regain her amateur status until 1945. She was a finalist that year, and Phyllis Otto was the champion.

During her short amateur career (1945–47), Babe won an incredible eighteen amateur titles. She wanted to play in amateur events, since prior to the formation of a professional tour, the Women's Western Open was the only national tournament a professional could enter. It was match play, with engraved silver artifacts for prizes. Babe believed women could play for money, so she returned to her professional standing and played in the fledgling Women's Professional Golf Association. In 1950 this organization became the Ladies Professional Golf Association. The formation of the LPGA brought the game for women to the forefront. It was the seed of acceptance for women playing the game.

Babe was an expert in promotion. She was a star, a great player, but above all, she was a great entertainer. She was the Tiger Woods of her era, with her booming drives. Instead of the long Scottish arm swing taught at the time, she powered the ball by using her hands to create immense club-head speed. The fans idolized her.

When she gave an exhibition, she would tell the gallery, "You walk down the fairway and see how far I hit the ball." Then she would walk back to the tee and stick a kitchen match in the ground behind her ball. When she hit it, there was a loud explosive crack and a flame would burst out. Galleries loved it.

When I was seventeen, as the Indiana State Junior champion, I was honored to be asked to play in an exhibition match with Babe. I was awed by her presence and her golf game, but she did everything she could to put me at ease. She laughed and joked with the large gallery, performed her match trick, and endeared herself to all.

Afterward, the promoters presented me with a watch trimmed with two small diamonds. I was worried about protecting my amateur standing, but Babe said, "Kid, put it on, wear it, and have a wonderful time. Don't be dumb." Since the Babe thought it was okay, I kept the watch, but I never wore it.

Learning the Rules

As an eighteen-year-old player, I did not know the rules as well as I should have. Playing in my first thirty-six-hole Indiana State Championship final, I had forged ahead after thirteen holes against my veteran opponent. The fourteenth was a long blind par three. It was customary for one player to send her caddie ahead to watch where the shots landed over the rise.

It was my honor, and my caddie walked ahead to be the spotter. He stood below the hill on my line of flight, and I shot over his head. My opponent waved him aside and then hit her shot. She then told me it was against the rules to use your caddie as an aiming point. She said I should know better and should lose the hole, but she was not going to enforce the rule. I offered to give her the hole. She refused but continued to make me feel guilty and miserable. I started to cry and could hardly see the ball through the tears, but I kept playing until I finished the eighteenth hole. Then I decided to quit even though I was nine up.

My father had watched the match from the gallery. He sat down beside me and said that quitting was not the correct way to handle the situation. He pointed out that I had not intended to break a rule and had offered to do the right thing. The rules officials approached and asked about the reason for my tears and then assured me that if the penalty had not been called at the end of the fourteenth hole, it was too late.

I sat with my father on the edge of the eighteenth green and tried to compose myself for the afternoon round. Should I continue in a childish sulk or go out and battle? I decided to play, and I won. From then on, I had my own rule: practice in the daytime—study the rulebook at night.

Years later, after many evenings with the rulebook, I was appointed chairman of the Rules Committee for an Indianapolis City Championship. It was reported to me that a promising young girl, playing in her first tournament, was unaware of tournament rules and inadvertently not in compliance.

The girl had a caddie, but neither had seen the course before. Her father, who was acquainted with the course, was walking with her and advising her where to aim from the tee. On every green, she changed her ball to putt with her "lucky putting ball." These infractions were finally called to her attention on the eighth tee. She then gave her bag to her father, making him her caddie, and she stopped changing her ball on the green.

After finishing her round, she brought her scorecard to me in the rules tent. I figured that she had played seven holes incurring a two-stroke penalty for each infraction, for a total of twenty-eight penalty strokes. Without penalties she had carded a 74. Adding all the penalty strokes would put her in the ninth flight—disastrous for her and perhaps her future in golf and equally unsatisfactory for the women in that flight.

Since she had asked only the direction in which to hit

the ball, instead of *how* to hit it, and changing the ball on the green was only an imaginary aid, I assessed her just two shots for each infraction under the USGA's Rule of Equity. Her score became 78, keeping her in the championship flight, where she belonged. She accepted this gratefully and finished runner-up in the championship. Ten years later, with full knowledge of all the rules, this player, Sandy Spuzich, became the USGA Women's Open champion.

While Sandy was attending college, I encouraged her to graduate before turning professional. She thanked me later, saying, "Every time I stand over a five-foot putt, I appreciate your insistence I earn a degree, because I say to myself . . . Hey, if I miss it, I can always earn a living teaching school."

Easy Money

Even though they were illegal, slot machines use to keep country clubs financially sound. The machines were tucked in the back of cloakrooms, but members and guests could duck in and play a few minutes or more.

As a teenager, I was fascinated with these slot machines. The desire to gamble was creeping into my soul. Somehow my father sensed this. One day when I was about fifteen, a state police car drove into our driveway. In the backseat, under wraps, was a confiscated slot machine my father had arranged to borrow.

My father asked the officers to put the slot machine in our recreation room. He gave me five dollars worth of nickels and the key to the back of the machine. I was so excited! Right away, I put a nickel in and pulled down the lever. No hit, but I saw the nickel drop into the jackpot window. I continued feeding the machine. When I finally scored a hit, two nickels fell into the cup at the bottom.

I played until I had fed the slot machine my entire supply of one hundred nickels. I wanted to continue playing, since I could see the jackpot window filling up. I unlocked and opened the back of the machine and found a cloth bag holding thirty nickels. I discovered that the slot machine had taken my one hundred nickels and diverted some into the jackpot window, some into the payoff for hits, and thirty into the owner's cloth bag. Realizing that eventually thirty of one hundred nickels ended up in the cloth bag in the back of the machine, it dawned on me that the owner of the machine was the winner, never the player. The fascination with slot machines was over. The spark of desire to gamble was extinguished. It went out completely and carried over to my golf game. Wagering on matches was never any fun. Just winning was enough for me.

His College—My College

When I was sixteen and competing in the Women's Western Golf Tournament, I met future golf great Peggy Kirk (Bell). She had just graduated from Rollins College in Winter Park, Florida, and was enthusiastic about the golf program there. I thought Peggy was wonderful and decided I wanted to follow in her footsteps: attend Rollins, improve my golf game, and become a member of her sorority, Kappa Kappa Gamma.

My father envisioned a different path for me. He had not had the opportunity to graduate from a prestigious Ivy League school and was determined that I should have an eastern college education. I presented my plea to attend Rollins with all kinds of reasons.

My parents knew nothing about Rollins. Their inquiries revealed that it was known as a tennis school teaching waterskiing and underwater basket weaving. This was not their idea of higher education, but my father finally offered me a deal. He agreed that if I could pass the entrance exams into Bryn Mawr, a college with the highest scholastic requirements, I could choose my college. Otherwise, he would select an eastern school for me.

During my junior year at the educationally acclaimed Shortridge High School, the entrance exams to colleges, including Bryn Mawr, were offered. After taking the tests, I waited anxiously for my fate. I passed, and my father kept his promise. At the age of seventeen, I would board the train with my golf clubs for Rollins College.

The only black cloud was the dreaded rush held by sororities during the first week before classes. I wanted to be a Kappa just like Peggy but feared they would not want me. Sororities had to participate in intramural sports, and my ability to play golf was instrumental to my becoming a Kappa. This was the first of many times in the future where my golf game would open a door for me.

Now I was a Kappa at Rollins, playing on the golf team, and to my father's delight, Rollins's academic standards were very high.

Gripping with Charms

World War II was ongoing, and the student body of Rollins was mostly female. The golf coach had been drafted, so I was asked to teach the women's physical education golf class.

Rollins had an arrangement with the Dubsdread Country Club to use their golf course and practice area. The club also opened their facilities to the cadets at the nearby

Naval Air station. Some played golf, but many hung out in the grillroom.

My class was full of girls who had no desire to learn golf but wanted to come to the clubhouse to flirt with the Naval Air cadets. My students all arrived for the golf class dressed in cute little outfits and with multiple charm bracelets dangling from their wrists. When I tried to show them how to grip the club, the charms slipped down between their hands and the club. Solution: Hold the club upright and then take a grip so the bracelets will slide down out of the way. Since I realized my students' true motivation, it was five swings, and the class was dismissed. The girls then headed for the clubhouse grill.

Rollins had a women's golf team, but the only competition was between sororities. Even after the war was over, we had no other college to compete against. Occasionally the men's golf team expanded their team when they played larger schools like the University of Miami. My good friend Lec Bongart (Hilkene) and I would play the number 7 and number 8 positions. We were not welcomed by opposing teams because we usually won!

Our senior year Lee and I paid our own way to the National Intercollegiate, held on the Scarlet Course of Ohio State University in Columbus. The format then was match play, but Lee and I won the two-man team medal event held during the eighteen-hole qualifying round. The Women's Intercollegiate has since changed the format to stroke play and has become one of the most prestigious tournaments in women's golf.

Alice quarterbacks Kappa sorority football team versus the Thetas at Rollins.

Hitting the Wall

Selecting mathematics as my college major was a disaster. During my second semester, I could not understand the problems, solutions, equations, or concepts. I had hit the wall. I had to change direction. It was not a question of defeat but one of realizing my brain was not functioning in that direction.

I changed my major to science and eventually graduated with honors and a bachelor of science degree in zoology. Little did I know that the amoebas I learned to draw would one day be the basis for the golf green shapes I drew on course routing plans for Pete.

My only regret is that I did not take vocational training in electronics, plumbing, and mechanics. I am sure Pete wished I had focused on cooking skills.

When you are trying to learn golf, "hitting the wall" can happen. There are many men and women teaching professionals using a variety of methods. If one confuses you, do not hit the wall and give up in despair. Change directions and find a professional you can understand.

Judge

F riends called my father "Judge," even though he was not a judge. He was very fair and could often settle disputes. I remember him telling me, "You are not always right. There are always two sides. If you go to a dinner party and you cannot get along with either one of the two people seated beside you, then it is not them, it is you."

When World War II began, two of my father's partners were called into the service. Upon their return, he made certain they were given their share of the firm's profits earned while they were serving their country. The two men received promotions as if they had been working there the entire time they were away.

My father taught me the importance of compromise. In my third year of college, I was upset by an incident I thought was unfair at my Kappa sorority. I was ready to resign. I wrote the reason to my father, and he responded with a wonderful and loving letter, explaining that quitting was never a solution. He said that even if I was right, it was more important to work things out or adjust to the situation than to quit. I took his advice, watched the situation resolve itself, and consequently managed to keep my sorority friends.

There have been many times during my golf career that I have wanted to quit. I have experienced unfair rulings, a committee reprimand, a referee timing me when I was not the slow one, and being bypassed for a team captaincy when I thought I deserved it. It was not always easy to swallow my pride and hurt feelings, but by heeding my father's wise advice, I have kept golf in my life.

*Alice's father, Perry O'Neal, hugs his daughter
after she wins the Indiana Women's Golf
Association Championship.*

Amateur or Professional

I graduated from Rollins in 1948. The LPGA had not yet been formed, and the only professionals I knew were Patty Berg and Babe Zaharias. I loved competing and played in the local Indianapolis City Championships and the Indiana State Championships. I would eventually win eleven city titles and nine state championships, but national championships were difficult to win.

In those tournaments, I had to compete against players such as Betsy Rawls, Louise Suggs, Mickey Wright, Kathy Whitworth, Carol Mann, Sandra Palmer, Sandra Spuzich, Judy Rankin, Hollis Stacy, Nancy Lopez, and Juli Inkster. They had not yet turned professional.

I was an amateur with no desire to play professionally. For me, golf was a sideline, not a vocation. I was pleased when many of the best amateur players joined the LPGA after it was formed in 1950. Now they were no longer competing against me in the amateur tournaments.

The status of women's golf in the 1950s is symbolized by the history of the Women's Open. It was first conducted in 1948 by the Women's Professional Golf Association and then by the LPGA from 1950 to 1952. In 1953 the USGA sponsored their first Open Championship at the Country Club of Rochester in upstate New York. There were thirty-seven entries. In 1954 entries rose to fifty-eight, but it took thirteen more years for the entries to reach one hundred.

Babe Zaharias won the event in 1948, 1950, and 1954, earning total prize money of $6,350. Mickey Wright won four Open Championships between 1958 and 1964, totaling $17,291 in prize money.

An amateur competing in the Open for any length of time is now the exception, not the rule. I played in twelve USGA Opens. I tied for twenty-fifth once, made the cut seven times, and had a stroke average of 80. Amateur Barbara McIntire, who lost in a play-off to Kathy Cornelius, had a stroke average of 77 in eight starts. She made five cuts. The only other amateur listed in the 2002 USGA media guide is Judy Bell, who once tied for fourteenth and had a stroke average of 80 for her five starts.

Both Barbara and Judy were good enough to compete professionally but chose to remain amateurs. They have been outstanding leaders and dedicated administrators of women's and men's golf.

Had there been the same opportunities when I was in my twenties as there are today for women professionals, I might have been tempted to play professionally. But back then even Patty Berg, Babe Zaharias, Betty Jameson, and other talented founding members had a struggle to keep the LPGA Tour alive.

Hooking Pete

In August 1945 World War II ended. The student body at Rollins College in Winter Park, Florida, began to return to normal, with equal numbers of men and women.

I first saw Pete Dye sitting at the counter of the food bar in the student union building. I thought he was really cute. I followed him through the cashier line but did not meet him until the next day, when I was surprised to see him on the practice tee at the Dubsdread Golf Course in Orlando.

*Pete and Alice during their college
days at Rollins.*

Somehow, I knew Pete was the one for me. He had just been discharged from the parachute infantry, and like many other servicemen, he wanted to have some fun. He turned the fire hose on his fellow members at a fraternity meeting, he won bets by jumping off a bridge onto the boxcar of a train and riding on the top to Tampa, but mostly he skipped class and played golf.

Undeterred by Pete's crazy antics, I had to figure out how to make him realize I was the one for him. It took three years, but finally in the spring of 1949, he came to my home in Indianapolis to propose . . . or so I thought.

My mother, anticipating the wedding of her only daughter, had designed a beautiful sunken garden. Pete planned to arrive Thursday and leave Sunday, so I arranged golf games for us with state champion Fred

Wampler and other outstanding amateurs. My parents were alerted that Pete would be asking for my hand in marriage.

Pete arrived as scheduled. We played Broadmoor, a Donald Ross masterpiece, where he shot 68. He followed that up with a great round of 69 at the Country Club of Indianapolis and then shot an impressive 68 at the Wood-stock Country Club on Sunday.

Afterward, we returned to my home, where my mother had little sandwiches for us on the pantry table. My parents sat in the upstairs sitting room, awaiting Pete's appearance. We enjoyed the sandwiches and then, without mentioning marriage, Pete prepared to leave. I gasped, "What about getting married?"

Heading out the door, he said, "Well, not in *golf season!*" and left.

There went my beautiful sunken-garden summer wedding. Fortunately, the cold Indiana winter came, ending the golf season, and Pete and I were married on Groundhog Day—February 2, 1950.

The ceremony almost did not take place. Standing at the top of the stairs, dressed in an elegant bridal gown and escorted by my father, I suddenly panicked. I told him, "I'm not going down."

My father's panic was probably worse than mine, but he calmly said, "Your mother has worked so hard to have a beautiful wedding. Her guests are all here, so for her sake, go down and go through with the ceremony, and I will annul it afterward."

The deal sounded fair, so we went down the stairs, and I became Alice O'Neal Dye. At our fiftieth anniversary celebration, I decided the annulment would not be necessary after all!

*The newlyweds dance at their
wedding reception.*

Bride's Cooking

Returning from our honeymoon, Pete and I moved into a one-bedroom, living room, and kitchen first-floor apartment.

Our parents helped us settle in and then left for a vacation in Florida. Before leaving, they suggested that it would be very nice if we invited a few of their friends for dinner. They left us a case of the finest scotch whisky to serve.

One Monday morning, after only a few weeks of marriage, I got up my nerve and called the wife of one of my parents' best friends, asking her if they could come to dinner *some* Thursday. Expecting a far-in-the-future acceptance, I was horrified when she cheerfully said the very next Thursday would be fine. I called another couple, and they also accepted for the next Thursday.

Panic! I called Pete at the office and asked him to bring home a chicken, while I studied a cookbook and pictures in magazines. Pete stopped at the city market, where they asked him if he wanted a New York–style hen. That sounded fancy, so he brought it home to me. Reaching inside to pull out the little sack of giblets, I screamed in shock when I hit the New York–style raw insides of that lady chicken.

Preparing for the arrival of our guests, I asked Pete to hang the mirror over our bedroom dresser. The nail he used went completely through the wall into the living room. He covered the protruding nail by hanging a washrag over it. Nouveau art! When our guests arrived, even though they were our parents' age, Pete made them take off their shoes because our rug was a wedding gift from his parents.

The dinner menu of chicken pot pie with biscuits and

a raw vegetable salad on a skewer had looked great in the magazine but did not quite turn out as I had planned. The chicken I cooked for three days was tough, the biscuits rock-hard, and the raw vegetables would not come off the skewer. Our guests drank lots of scotch whisky to wash it all down.

Pete and I did not drink coffee, so I had no idea how to make it. I perked a pot in the morning, reperked it in the afternoon, and again right before serving it. The coffee poured out like syrup. Our guests asked if it was chicory and opted for more scotch.

Later in the evening, the guests politely and a little drunkenly thanked us for a lovely time. They found their shoes, left, and on the way home probably recanted the disasters of their own first dinner party.

I looked at the remains of our dinner and knew that cooking, like golf, would take a lot of practice.

Houses

After honeymooning eight months in an apartment, we moved into a three-bedroom brick house on a quiet residential street. We were golfers and knew nothing of homemaking or yard keeping, nor did we have time to devote to either.

Pete, Alice, P. B., Perry, and
Blackie during the Christmas
season, circa 1959.

Pete was greens chairman of the Country Club of Indianapolis and was gradually annihilating their fairways with his experiments. At one point, the brown half of the first fairway was known as "the Dye half."

Not wanting to have to cut our front yard every week, Pete decided to let it grow and reseed itself. All our neighbors had neatly trimmed yards, while we had a hayfield. Pete finally had to cut it with a scythe. Every time I suggested new wallpaper or carpeting, Pete would tell me, "What was good enough for Odie [Odie Chrisman, the previous owner] is good enough for me."

Eight years later we built a one-story ranch-style house with a large front yard on the north side of Indianapolis. Pete was planting trees at the Country Club of

Indianapolis, so he tried planting several large ones in our front yard. Shocked by the move, they stood almost leafless for five years.

In the front yard of this home we grew the bent grass for our first golf course. Here stood the giant yellow tractor Pete bought instead of the mink coat he promised me. We named the tractor "Mother's Mink."

Our young sons, Perry and P. B., began their architecture careers driving Mother's Mink in the front yard. They used the tractor attachments to move dirt around and shape mounds, bunker pits, and even a dirt racetrack.

Ten years later we moved to Florida and bought a thirty-year-old one-story house in a very sedate neighborhood. We decided the house needed painting, so we selected a pale yellow color. Trusting our color selection, we left for the day to play golf when the painters arrived. Returning late that afternoon, we were shocked to see our new home was a brilliant yellow. It looked like a Midas Muffler store.

Our neighbors were rightfully horrified. Pete's petite mother, Elizabeth, was flying back to her Delray Beach home when the lady seated next to her politely asked if she lived in Florida. As the conversation progressed, the lady said that she had a winter home in a lovely area, but these awful people had moved into the neighborhood. She continued complaining, saying the couple had a red truck, two teenage boys, two white German shepherd dogs, and had painted their home a bilious yellow. Elizabeth smiled in mock sympathy.

In 1990 Anton (Tony) George, owner of the famous Indianapolis Motor Speedway, approached Pete about remodeling his eighteen-hole golf course. Thirty years earlier, Pete, Richard Stackhouse, and Tom Moses had been the originators and promoters for a PGA Tour tournament played on the Speedway golf course. The only other PGA event ever played in Indianapolis, many years earlier, had been dubbed the Rubber Check Open because an October date and bitterly cold weather triggered a scarcity of cash to pay the promised purse. This new 1960 May event at the Speedway golf course was to be played Thursday through Sunday, but in a departure from the PGA Tour's eighteen-hole play-off, if needed, there was to be a "sudden death" play-off to avoid a conflict with Monday's race. The purse was $50,000, the largest ever for a regular PGA event.

Tickets were $7 for seven days, and large crowds of race fans camping out near the entrance to the track were expected to come. It was a shock and a surprise that the race fans, even at the low ticket fare, ignored Arnold Palmer, Gary Player, and Billy Casper, all participating in the tournament inside the Speedway gates. The sudden-death play-off was needed, as Arnold Palmer eagled the eighteenth hole to tie Doug Ford but then bogeyed the first play-off hole to lose. The usually quiet atmosphere players demanded was often broken by the loud whine of practicing racecars.

As the purse increased, the PGA found more lucrative venues, and the Speedway needed more infield space. The nine holes inside the track were removed and redesigned by Bill Diddle to meld with the nine on the outside.

When Tony George engaged Pete to redesign the course in 1990, Pete was excited. He had been a part owner of a racecar, and he loved the history of the Speedway and the golf course. He wanted to create something very special for his good friend Tony and once again position some of the golf holes inside the racetrack. Pete designed four holes inside the famed oval, and Tony named the course Brickyard Crossing, signifying the crossing of the racetrack. Golfers who play there are treated to a championship venue while sometimes hearing the roar of racecars practicing for the Indy 500, Nascar's Brickyard 400, or the Formula One race.

Knowing Pete would be very involved in this project and that Crooked Stick would host the PGA Championship in 1991 and the USGA Women's Open in 1993, I assumed we would be spending more than our usual time visiting the Indianapolis area.

With this in mind, I told Pete I would like to have a house in Indianapolis. He said, "What for?" When our new home bordering the eighteenth hole of Crooked Stick was completed, we called it "Casa What For."

Babes in the Dirt

Prior to becoming a golf course designer, Pete was a very successful life insurance salesman. He was a member of the Million Dollar Round Table and was on schedule to become head of the Indianapolis Connecticut Mutual Life Insurance Agency.

Pete had won the Indiana State Amateur Championship. I was the mother of our two young children, Perry and P. B., and the winner of several Indiana State championships and many local events. We both served on United States Golf Association committees and boards of the Men's and Women's Western Golf Associations. We had built a house on seven acres on the outskirts of Indianapolis. Life was on track.

I was stunned when Pete arrived home one evening and said he was bored with the insurance business. What he really wanted us to do was design and build golf courses. Financially we could take a risk, as his insurance business had a good compensation from renewals.

At the time, the golf course architecture profession was so small and unrecognized that we knew of only two men who built courses: Robert Trent Jones and William Diddle. We figured the best way to get started would be to work for one of them.

Mr. Jones owned the Coral Ridge Country Club on

the northern outskirts of Fort Lauderdale, Florida. It hosted the Doherty Jones Women's Golf Championship, which I competed in each January.

Mr. Jones always attended the elegant buffet dinner the club gave for all the contestants. I thought this would be an ideal time to approach him about hiring us.

After dinner, Mr. Jones was seated in a large lounge chair, and I sat on the floor at his feet and asked if he would hire us. He said, "Yes, but not in the design department." We both smiled as I shook my head.

Our next plan was to visit Mr. Diddle, a noted Indiana architect and a founding member of the American Society of Golf Course Architects. We knew nothing about the American Society of Golf Course Architects or that he and Mr. Jones had both been founding members. Years later both Pete and I would each serve as president of that prestigious society and reluctantly remodel Mr. Diddle's Woodland Golf Course.

Mr. Diddle lived in a small rustic log cabin nestled in the woods of his Woodland Country Club in Carmel, Indiana. We had great respect for Mr. Diddle and would have loved to work for him. When we visited him in his cabin, he said he could not hire us, since he was retiring. He discouraged us, saying golf course architecture was financially a very risky business. Two strikeouts—and then my attorney father told Pete that because he did not have a degree in architecture, he could not call himself a golf course architect and must use the title of golf course designer. Strike three.

In spite of all these discouragements and the fact that records of the time indicated that very few new courses were being built in the United States each year, we did not give up. Only two real innocents would have dared to enter the field of golf course architecture.

Our First Course

Alice starts building bunkers atop a bulldozer.

After much advertising, word-of-mouth appeals, frustration, and several false starts, Pete and I finally were asked to build a course on the south side of Indianapolis.

Our heads throbbed with ideas gleaned from playing tournaments on famous courses. We wanted to incorporate the surround swales of Pinehurst, the double fairways of Chicago's Shore Acres, the undulating greens of Oakland Hills, the bunkering of Carmargo, and the strategies of Donald Ross's Scioto. All this in only nine holes!

As members of the USGA committees, we wanted to build the first USGA greens ever constructed. On top of all that, we became fascinated with the potential of using, for the first time, plastic pipe introduced to us by Paul O'Cane, who explained its merits to me in a barbershop while my sons were getting their hair cut.

We nearly broke the owner with our determination to build a great nine holes incorporating all these features. We paid no attention to the type of middle-income housing project he was planning but proceeded to build a very difficult championship layout.

Our owner was a contractor who knew nothing about golf or golf courses. He did not realize the severity of multiple creek crossings or the complex green contours we were constructing. I decided to move the dirt myself but quickly discovered that his foot-controlled bulldozer was way beyond my leg strength.

Our front yard became the nursery for raising the bent grass for the greens. The three sons of our friends Judy and Taylor Wilson were in charge of weeding. When the bent grass was established, it was verticut and the stolons loaded into large burlap bags and crammed into the trunk of my black Oldsmobile. The weight made the car so rear heavy, the front wheels barely touched the pavement. I felt like I was driving a motorboat as I transported the bags from our house twenty miles south to the course that would be known first as El Dorado and later as Royal Oak.

The homegrown bent grass stolons were cast upon the first nine USGA greens ever built. They grew and still thrive today. When the course opened successfully, Pete and I became "golf course designers."

The Second Course

Soon after our first nine-hole course opened, a local developer approached Pete and me with a proposition to build an eighteen-hole course. He had only eighty-four acres for the course and a low budget. The clubhouse and parking lot would be adjoining and not included in the limited area of land.

Eager and undaunted, we accepted his proposal to build the course known then as Heather Hills and now as Maple Creek. Pete walked the flat land, which featured a winding creek and a few trees. I drew up a map with eighteen holes and a practice area.

We began August 1 and had perfect weather—not a drop of rain. We were both on site every day and in six weeks had shaped tees, greens, bunkers, and mounds and were ready to seed.

The earth was so dry it was like dusty powder. We sowed the seed, and the next day a gentle misty rain began, followed by several days of light rainfall. Within one week the seed sprouted, and soon the green fuzz became grass. Three months from conception we had a golf course and our $8,000 fee. We were lured into thinking that this was an easy profession.

The following spring, the chairman of the club's ladies committee telephoned me in Florida to say she had walked the course and could find only seventeen holes. Pete panicked, but I was sure I had drawn eighteen holes and we had planted eighteen greens. I told the lady chairman to be sure the club had bought eighteen flagsticks. If the superintendent could not find a green for each of them, we would just stay in Florida. It turned out one par three was so short, she had skipped it.

A Foolish Promise

When Perry was eight and P. B. was five, we accompanied Pete and his golf partner, Wayne Timberman Jr., to Cincinnati, Ohio. They were entered in a two-man best ball at the exclusive Losantiville Country Club.

While they were competing, I took our young boys to the fabulous Cincinnati Zoo. We saw many beautiful animals—giraffes, lions, elephants, and monkeys, creatures that would normally capture the attention of boys—but it was the pigeons strutting around the walkways that fascinated young P. B. He said, "Mom, if I catch a pigeon, may I keep it?" I promised he could, since I knew it is absolutely impossible to catch a zoo pigeon. They are used to crowds of people, and those pigeons will allow a person nearby to feed them but then quickly scoot away.

The boys and I headed for the corn machine, where a nickel would dispense a handful of corn. P. B. put in the coin and caught the corn in his little hand. He tried in vain to bait the savvy pigeons. Not willing to give up, he asked for more corn. He put another nickel in the machine but did not get his hand underneath the dispenser in time to catch the grains of corn. All of the kernels dropped to the cement. An eager pigeon scampered under the machine to eat the corn, but P. B.'s little hand was right there, and he grabbed it. He caught a pigeon! I could not believe it. The chance of this actually happening was so remote, I had not even considered what I would do if he was successful. Excited, P. B. began asking for a cage for his prize. We left the zoo with the pigeon held tightly in his hands, drove to the nearest pet shop, and bought a large cage. There I was with two bedraggled boys and a caged pigeon on my way to pick up Pete and Wayne at the very formal country club.

P. B. did not want to leave his pigeon in the parked car, so he and Perry struggled to carry the wire cage into the country club. What a foursome we were—a haggard mother with two disheveled boys lugging a large cage containing an unhappy pigeon. We walked to the scoreboard area where players were congregating, garnering many curious smiles and chuckles along the way. I spotted Pete. He and Wayne were being congratulated on their good round. I motioned him over. He took one look at our motley crew and said, "I'll meet you in the car."

P. B. was so proud of capturing the pigeon that I was thankful I kept my word to him despite my personal discomfort. Think before you promise, but promises should be kept.

Zookeeper

Growing up, my mother and father allowed me all kinds of pets: a little Shetland pony named Mary Jane, a cuddly blond cocker spaniel named Sugar, unnamed turtles, fish, birds, and even a cage full of white rats. Continuing the tradition of this mini zoo, our sons owned raccoons, dogs, cats, turtles, a pigeon, frogs, baby chicks, and ducklings.

One Christmas when we were living in Florida, Perry's gift to P. B. topped them all. In a double-lidded, old-fashioned wicker basket was a big, fat, healthy twelve-foot boa constrictor. P. B. was overjoyed. I was less than thrilled. The snake would hang from the rafter in P. B.'s room, ensuring his complete privacy.

P. B. would take his white German shepherd dog, Gypsy, on a leash, carry his wicker hamper concealing the boa constrictor, and stroll down the dock to his motorboat moored at the nearby senior citizen yacht club. The elderly bystanders would comment how cute he looked with his dog and hamper of snacks. Little did they know.

Eventually, I persuaded P. B. to share his snake with his classmates. Much to my relief and to the horror of his teacher, Mr. Boa Constrictor went to St. Andrew's School for the remainder of his life.

Sam Snead Says . . .

Every man should learn to cook, sew, and garden.
—Sam Snead

Our sons were taught to cook as soon as they were old enough to stand on a chair and stir cake batter. One of the toughest things I ever had to do was watch eight-year-old P. B. sew up his ripped football pants. I wanted so badly to do it for him, but he learned by doing it himself. Both boys have become master gardeners as well. Sam would approve.

Perry began hitting golf balls before he was three and progressed to lead the golf team at Winchington School in Boston, Massachusetts. When P. B. was ten, he had hit hundreds of golf balls on the practice range but had little playing experience. Pete, wanting him to learn to play on the course, offered him a deal. If he would play twenty-five rounds of nine holes each, Pete would buy him a new bicycle.

With his little bag and a few clubs, P. B. played nine holes, keeping a running score as he progressed. After each shot, he added one to his score—25, 26, or 27, and so forth—instead of posting a score for each hole and adding it up at the end of the round. P. B. earned his

*Sam Snead presents Alice with the
championship trophy at the
1966 Greenbriar Festival.*

bicycle and eventually became a scratch handicapper, playing in national tournaments.

Both boys often abandoned their golf clubs when we began constructing golf courses. They loved the mechanical equipment and operated sand pros, tractors, and small bulldozers. Construction crept into their hearts.

After college, both Perry and P. B. expressed their desire to become golf course architects, and we wanted to help them get started. The problem was deciding who should join us for what projects. The Mississippi River provided a good divider. Perry, who lived in Denver, worked with Pete and me on projects west of the river, while P. B. took the projects to the east. Both boys soon became independent, and we are very proud of them and the courses they have designed and constructed. Perry and P. B. are both members of the prestigious American Society of Golf Course Architects. They both can cook and garden, but only P. B. can sew.

(from top right to left) Golf course designers P. B. Dye, Perry Dye, and Pete and Alice Dye in American Society of Golf Course Architects Ross plaid jackets.

The Bandit

During golf course construction in the spring, we often found baby raccoons that had been abandoned when we had to cut down a tree that harbored their nest.

One evening, Pete brought P. B. a little six-inch-long baby raccoon. P. B. named him Racky and fed him with an eyedropper. As Racky grew, P. B. kept him on his shoulder or wrapped around his neck.

A young raccoon learns life by imitating its mother, so Racky followed his foster mother P. B. everywhere, including the dinner table. Raccoons have no salivary glands and must dip their food in water before putting it

P. B. with Racky the raccoon.

in their mouths, so we provided a little bowl of water beside his plate.

Racky was a very tidy eater; he sat right next to P. B. until he was finished and then crawled back on P. B.'s shoulder. At night when checking on P. B. in bed sleeping, I could see the little boy shape under the covers and then, clear down at the bottom of the bed, a tiny mound—Racky.

One summer afternoon my mother gave me one of her rings. It was a beautiful square-cut emerald. I was delighted with it and sat on our couch wearing it, waving my hand and catching flashing rays of sun shining through the window. Racky, almost grown, was watching.

Wanting to keep the ring safe, I took it to my bedroom, opened the top dresser drawer, lifted the lid of my jewelry box, placed the ring in the box, and locked it, leaving the little key in the keyhole. I then closed the dresser drawer and went to the kitchen to start dinner.

A bit later, I returned to the bedroom and was shocked to see my dresser drawer pulled out and the jewelry box open. The ring was gone. No one had entered the house, so I knew Racky had to be the culprit.

Raccoons are not called "little bandits" for nothing. I had read that raccoons usually steal something, hide it nearby, and then come back later to take it to their nest. Quickly, I closed all the doors to the outside and began a panicked search. I looked under the bed, behind the pillows, below the bedside tables, and beneath the chairs, all without any luck. Finally, I moved the tall corner chest and spied the ring, totally hidden behind the back leg.

You cannot scold a raccoon, so the ring went to the safety deposit box. As much as P. B. loved Racky, he knew that when autumn came, Racky must be returned to the wild. Racky knew it too and took off to be with his own.

Advice from Barbara Nicklaus

It is routine for a woman to be torn between leaving on a short business trip with her husband or staying home with the children. Either decision creates guilt. It is the age-old problem of wanting to be in two places at once.

Barbara Nicklaus once wrote a meaningful article for a popular women's magazine explaining that when she could obtain competent care for her children, it was a priority to go for a few days to support Jack. Her rationale was that she was a mother but also a wife, and she should be there for her husband whenever she could.

Barbara loved her children more than anything, but she made time for Jack. She walked in his gallery—not inside the ropes on the fairway, where it was easy. She trudged outside the ropes over mounds, around trees, in high grasses, and through his large gallery. She did it to support Jack, and I know it meant a great deal to him.

Barbara's wisdom helped me decide to travel with Pete to some of our construction sites. To make parting easier, we always gave our young sons a going-away present, eliminating the rushed airport purchase on the way home.

One year we gave each of the boys a kitten. One was tabby colored, and the other one was white with a black spot. When we arrived home, the boys told us they had named the kittens Scotch and Martini. We said that was very clever, as one was the color of scotch, and the black spot on the white kitten could be an olive in a martini. "No, Mom and Dad," they explained. "That is not why we named them Scotch and Martini. It is because that is what you always say to your guests—scotch or martini?" Those kittens became monster cats and lived a happy life before going to cat heaven.

Pass It On

My father and mother helped many people, but they always did it anonymously. Having parents who gave to others set a good example for me. When anyone tried to repay them, my parents always said, "Pass it on to someone you know who needs help."

Many of the young men who worked for Pete and me are now professional golf course designers and members of the American Society of Golf Course Architects. Some joined us with no experience. Many started by picking up sticks or working on the construction crews, but for those who worked hard and wanted to learn, we provided an opportunity.

When we were beginning to start construction on the Long Cove on Hilton Head Island, South Carolina, Pete reluctantly interviewed a young assistant superintendent who came highly recommended. Pete really did not want to hire anyone as project superintendent, as he preferred to be hands-on and do the job himself. I liked the young man and felt he could really help Pete and allow him more time for his other course-construction commissions.

Pete agreed to give this young man a try, but when construction started and he showed up wearing a starched white shirt, pressed khakis, and polished shoes and carrying a clipboard, Pete complained, "This kid is worthless." But as time went on, Pete worked with him and explained how he wanted things done. Soon, the young man got down in the ditches and got his shirt dirty, his pants filthy, donned heavy work boots, learned to use all of the heavy equipment, and discarded the clipboard. The young man was Bobby Weed, who became an outstanding course designer and a member of the American Society of Golf Course Architects. Now Bobby is passing on his knowledge to those young men who work for him.

A cocky young redheaded kid used to caddie for us at the Country Club of Indianapolis. When the time arrived for him to go to college, he came to us for some financial help. Knowing him to be very industrious, we were glad to help a little. After he had graduated from college and worked as a golf professional, and then later as a golf course owner, Mickey Powell came to repay the debt. We said, "Pass it on." He repaid every penny and said, "You pass it on." Mickey Powell became president of the PGA of America and has "passed it on" to so many others.

When to Start Kids Playing Golf

Hit 'em hard—they'll land somewhere.
—Steward Maiden

Golf guru Harvey Penick said, "The best age to start a child in golf is the time he or she becomes interested in the game. If a child four or five years old is eager to go out and play with mom or dad, then it is time to start."

As Penick suggests, kids should begin at an early age, since they are not as self-conscious as teenagers become.

Parents ought to take their child and a pal to the driving range and just let them hit the balls. Golf can be a lonely game, so having a friend helps. Teaching professional Peggy Kirk Bell said, "There are only two things about teaching children to play golf that are important. One, get their grip right from the beginning. Two, let them have fun." Make sure kids do not get upset or try too hard. Five whiffs and one connect is just fine.

When you take youngsters to the golf course, start them from the 150-yard marker. From there, they can see the green and the flagstick and have a chance of making "par." They do know about par and what it means. Cart lap driving to the 150-yard marker is probably just as much fun for a child as golf. Just remember, even an unattended two-year-old can start a cart. Take the key!

Andy Coogan

While Pete and I were traveling through Scotland, attempting to learn the design features of the great courses, we had all kinds of interesting caddies. They were usually men who had caddied for years at their course and loved the game.

When we arrived at Carnoustie, our caddies were young lads about fourteen years old. They were bundled from head to knees in heavy dark coats. My caddie, Andy Coogan, was chipper, enthusiastic, and all boy. I was charmed.

Between golf and camera shots, I asked Pete what he thought about inviting my caddie to visit us in the United States. Not thinking I was really serious, he kept playing the course and thinking of the great shots Ben Hogan made at Carnoustie in 1953 to win the British Open.

I asked Andy if he would like to come to the United States. Completing our round, we waited for Andy to speak to his family. Shortly thereafter, they came to the clubhouse to arrange for the trip. Pete was blindsided but agreed to Andy's arrival in America the next month.

Young Andy had never even been in an automobile before, but we made all his travel arrangements, and he arrived safely at the Indianapolis airport, carrying only a small satchel.

After a welcoming lunch, our first trip was to the mall for clothes—shorts, T-shirts, underwear, socks, the works—and he became a member of our family. We enrolled him in a local high school as a freshman.

Andy had no high school experience because at that time Scotland had an educational system that ended after the eighth grade unless a student had exceptional grades and was dedicated to learning. Andy was quite bright, but he had wanted to caddie instead of study. However, he did well in our school. His good looks and Scottish brogue attracted quite a few of the girls. In the summer, Andy worked in the Meridian Hills golf shop for professional Wayne Timberman Sr.

After two years with us, it was time for Andy to return to Scotland and his family. He departed with new clothes, a new set of golf clubs, and enough money and desire to continue his education.

Years passed, and our contact with Andy diminished. We did know that he had continued his education, graduated, and immigrated to Australia to work for the Timex watch company.

To further enhance our knowledge of great golf courses, Pete and I traveled to New Zealand and Australia. We timed our visit to coincide with the Australian Open, where our friends Curtis Strange and Bobby Clampett were competing. While walking in the huge gallery following the American players, who should appear out of the crowd but Andy! We recognized him immediately, even though he was now thirty-five years old and sporting a bushy mustache.

What a reunion we enjoyed. Andy was a real business success and now working for the Seiko watch company. He was a member of the prestigious Victoria Country Club.

Pete and Alice with Andy Coogan,
their "adopted" Scottish son.

The Melbourne newspaper learned of Andy's story, and the next day, photographs of the three of us and a long article about the reunion were prominently displayed.

After several days of playing golf and dining together, Pete and I were scheduled to return home. Andy pulled me aside and said he noticed Pete was not wearing a watch. Andy said he had some samples to show me. I picked out a really nice one, thinking it was to be a gift, but Andy, a Scotsman to the core, offered it to me *wholesale!*

Pete wore the timepiece, calling it his $20,000 watch, referring to Andy's expenses while in our care.

Cut to the Rubber

During the 1977 USGA Women's Senior Amateur Championship at the Rancho Bernardo Golf Club near San Diego, California, the temperature was 112 degrees. My steel shafts were too hot to touch.

With one round to play, I led by eight strokes. By the end of nine holes, my good friend Cecile Maclaurin had shot 34 and cut my lead to four. Protecting a lead is the most difficult way to play. Somehow you change the way you played to get the lead.

By the seventeenth hole I was one shot behind, but Cecile, playing in the group ahead of me, found trouble on her finishing hole. I learned that if I could par my eighteenth hole, I would win by a stroke.

The fairway on the par-five eighteenth hole was narrow, and I tried to steer my drive to safety. Instead, I guided it left out of bounds into someone's swimming pool. Devastated and angry at my mistake, I grabbed another ball from my bag, re-teed, and furiously lashed a really long, straight drive.

Hitting my second and third shots with emotional energy, I was eventually fifteen feet from the hole. If I could make the putt, I would tie, and there would be an eighteen-hole play-off the next day.

I marked, cleaned, and replaced the ball while staring

at the line to the hole. I addressed the ball, held my head steady, and saw my putter hit the ball. When I looked up, the ball was rolling on line, and it fell into the cup.

As I leaned over to take the ball out of the cup, I was stunned to see that it was cut to the rubber. The flawless first ball was in someone's swimming pool, but this deeply damaged ball had not messed up a shot. If I had noticed the deep gash and realized I had pulled a slashed ball out of my bag, the rules would not have permitted a change. My confidence would have been shattered. I would not have tied Cecile and gone on to win the eighteen-hole play-off to become the USGA Senior Women's Amateur champion.

Big Mama

JoAnne Gunderson Carner, "Big Mama," is one of golf's great entertainers. She is also as fierce a competitor as the game has ever seen. During our semifinal match of the USGA Women's Amateur Championship at the Prairie Dunes Country Club in Hutchinson, Kansas, JoAnne hit her ball on the seventh hole into a shallow bunker close to a yucca plant.

One of the features at Prairie Dunes is large yucca

plants. They are about three feet tall, with stiff, swordlike spikes. JoAnne's ball was practically in the plant, so I figured it was unplayable. I had already reached the green with my second shot and assumed I would win the hole. Then I watched in horror as JoAnne, clad in shorts, backed into the yucca plant. I thought I was going to die watching. The sharp, pointed spears inched into her back and cut her legs. She steadied herself and hit a fabulous shot to the green. I just could not believe that she had the determination to back into such agony. She easily won our match.

JoAnne is a great player. She plays for the pin, no matter where it is. Galleries love her; other players love her. She is a star who loves playing the game and shows it.

Curtis Cup

Golf is my game and I love it. If I had to, I'd play it with rocks.
—Margaret Curtis

The crowning achievement for every woman amateur golfer is selection to the Curtis Cup Team. Begun in 1932 by sisters Margaret and Harriot Curtis, the Cup is a competition between two teams of eight players from

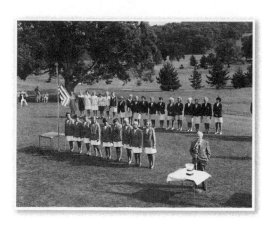

*Alice with her teammates at the 1970 Curtis Cup
flag-raising ceremony.*

the United States versus Great Britain, Ireland, and
Wales. Every two years, the teams compete in matches for
two days.

The format is a foursome (alternate shot) and singles.
The USGA Women's Committee selects the U.S. team
through computation of a player's performance over the
previous two years. All events count, but USGA events are
the most significant. There is no age or location limit, but
the one selected must be a citizen of the United States.

Making this team was my goal—not always a priority
but always a goal. In every national tournament I played,
there was always the pressure of doing well to make the
team. Standing over a putt, instead of concentrating on
holing it, I stupidly would think that if I made it, I might
be considered for the team. I never gave up and finally

started concentrating on sinking my putts instead of making the team, and I won the Eastern, the North and South, the Doherty, and made a good showing in the USGA tournaments. At forty-three years old, I received that long-awaited call from the USGA, inviting me to be on the 1970 Curtis Cup Team.

Soon my gold pin and red, white, and blue uniforms began arriving, and then it was time to board the airplane for Boston. I was so delighted that we were playing in the United States that year, because my father, Pete, fifteen-year-old P. B., and eighteen-year-old Perry could come to watch.

After four days of practice with my much younger teammates, it was time for the flag-raising ceremony. As the national anthem played and our flag was being raised, I was so overcome with emotion that I had to hold onto a teammate to keep from collapsing to the ground. The next day, the matches began, and I was to play the afternoon singles. My teammates experienced a tough morning with the foursomes—an alternate-shot match we seldom played—and the United States was behind.

As the anchor for the singles match, I had to wait a long morning and part of the afternoon for my three o'clock tee time. When it was finally time to hit my opening tee shot, I felt as if all the blood had drained from my body. Fortunately, the first tee was elevated, so my feeble drive at least became airborne.

Regaining my composure, I played on, but I was two holes down with three holes to play when team captain Caroline Cudone approached and asked how I was doing. Upon learning the status of my match, she grimaced and said, "You *have* to win."

I strode up the hill to my pitch shot to the sixteenth hole with renewed determination and won that hole and the next with perfect shots. All tied at the eighteenth tee, I was so pumped up that I powered my drive thirty yards past my usual landing area, hit the green with a long iron, and putted up three feet from the cup. If I holed my putt, I would win my match. I can still see the line today and my putter going back low and slow and then watching the blade hit the ball. Holding my head and eyes steady, I could not see the hole. It seemed like forever before I heard the winning putt hit the bottom of the cup and my teammates cheering and clapping. My match was a turning point in the competition, and we went on to win the Curtis Cup.

Turn Back

The threat of polio is now a distant memory, but the crippling disease was a haunting concern until the Salk vaccine proved effective.

As a young mother, I received one of the first batches

of Cutter Company's vaccine. It proved to be too active and resulted in a poliolike symptom in my left side. Advised by doctors to avoid the cold weather, I rented a house for our family during the winter months in Delray Beach, Florida. Tommy Armour, a native of Scotland and nicknamed the Silver Scot, was also living in Delray.

Each day, Mr. Armour, who won the 1927 USGA Open, went to the Delray Beach Municipal Golf Club, where he sat in a king-size chair with a table of his friends. After several cups of coffee chased with Bromo Seltzers, he walked to the practice tee.

From a folding seat, Mr. Armour gave free lessons to select followers. Luckily I was included, and my long,

*The sweet swing that produced
birdies and championships
galore.*

loose arm swing was transformed into one with more hand action.

In an effort to control my long backswing, I began to shorten my shoulder turn. Golf is a game of opposites. Tommy Armour said to me, "You can overswing, but you cannot overturn."

As I increased my shoulder turn back, my backswing became shorter. When I wanted to hit it longer, I just made a bigger turn back.

Dye Three-Putt Rule

Three-putting the first green of your round can set a bad tone for your whole day. When we were first married, Pete and I were members of the Country Club of Indianapolis. The par-four starting hole had an elevated tee, then sharply descended down to the fairway, leaving a good drive some 200 yards from the large green. In those days, it took a well-struck two-iron to hit a ball 200 yards.

Pete would hit a big drive and a great two-iron and reach the green—off to a good start to shoot a low score. If he then three-putted, he would look at me and say, "Let's start over." We would walk all the way back up to the first tee and play the hole again.

The third time I was trudging up the hill to the first tee I said, "New rule—you can't three-putt the first green." Pete endorsed the idea, and for years now, the Dye "can't three-putt the first green" rule has helped us, as well as our friends, get off to a good start in casual rounds.

Trouble to Trouble

My good friend Robin Weiss Donnelley has developed into a champion golfer, winning national tournaments and being selected as a member of the Curtis Cup Team three times. But when she first began playing in tournaments, she would fail to qualify for the championship flight because double and triple bogeys ate up her birdies and elevated her score. A bogey can offset a birdie, but a double bogey takes away two birdies, and a triple bogey destroys three birdies.

When Robin and I were at the Mid Pines Resort in Southern Pines, North Carolina, practicing for the Women's Southern Amateur Championship, Robin asked me to play a practice round with her and make any suggestions on better course management that would help her to post lower scores. On the first hole, her drive found a high-lipped bunker. I said, "Robin—you are in trouble. Do not go from trouble to trouble. Find the 150-yard marker and pitch out to there, since you know you can reach the green and maybe one-putt or, at worst, two-putt. You will be playing for par and one-half." She pitched out and recorded a bogey.

Robin birdied the second hole, and on the third hole, her drive bounced into the woods. I kept her from trying a miracle shot toward the green and probably going from "trouble to trouble" by again suggesting that she find the 150-yard marker and pitch out to it.

The idea of simply pitching out to the area of the 150-yard marker is very difficult for a strong player, but Robin complied and made a bogey. I stayed near her, always saying, "Do not go from trouble to trouble," and her round was going well. On the eighteenth hole, after four hours of stressing management, I snap-hooked my drive into the left woods. Robin pushed hers off into the trees on the right. While hunting for my ball, I heard a tremendous rattling of leaves as Robin tried a miracle shot. No miracle occurred, and she dumped her ball into a deep bunker. I yelled over, "Robin, you went from trouble to trouble!" She grinned and said, "It slipped my mind."

Robin qualified in championship flight that year and has gone on to win the Women's Southern Amateur three times, two USGA Mid Amateurs, and numerous other important tournaments.

Practice

Practice puts brains in your muscles.

—Sam Snead

Victory is the culmination of preparation. I used to practice, spending hours alone on the course, the range, the practice bunker, the chipping green, and finally the putting green. It was lonely sometimes, but practice provided the confidence that gave commitment to my shots.

When I begin to practice, I like to check my notes on past sessions and then start swinging gently and fully with a lofted utility wood. These swings are really back muscle stretches and extended turns back and through. I then start hitting balls with a seven-iron—little shots, increasing my backswing and follow-through. I want to feel my weight shift to the inside of the right foot and then completely over to the left side, finishing with the right toe pointed down. Only after feeling my swing flowing do I move to longer clubs.

I save the wedge shots for the pitching green and bunker, as there is no weight shift on these short shots. I do not want to practice them first and get in the habit of not shifting my weight for the longer clubs.

If I am warming up before playing a round, I start the same way with stretches, then the seven-iron, working up to the driver. The big problem is moving your practice tee swing to the first tee. One day before a match, I was walking from the practice range to the first tee in little baby steps. When someone asked me what was wrong with my legs, I said I was just trying to get to the first tee without changing anything.

Why does a beautiful, effective golf swing change from the practice range to the first tee? How can a few minutes' walk restrict my turn, tighten my grip, freeze my legs, and put fear in my brain? It happens. What to do: Expect it. Deal with it by remembering the rhythm of your practice tee swing and focusing on contact with the ball.

Lessons

At seventy-five years old, I still wanted to play well, but I had let several years slip by, thinking I was too busy or too tired for a lesson. Instead, I had opted for a quick fix from Pete or my golf friends. Finally I realized it was time to see a real professional.

After contacting PGA professional Mark Mielbrecht at our Florida club, Gulf Stream Golf Club, I told him the story of my friend Ann Moses. She had called her friend, a highly respected orthopedic surgeon, for help with a bad cold. He suggested rest and maybe some aspirin, but her condition worsened, so she called him again. This time, he ordered a prescription for cold medicine. A few days later, she was on his doorstep with a really bad cold, begging for help. The esteemed orthopedic surgeon said, "Ann, why don't you go to a *real doctor?*"

I told Mark I now needed a *real professional* and asked if he could help me. He smiled and said, "I will check my lesson book and call you." An hour later my answering machine related, "This is Dr. Mark, your orthopedic golf coach, and I will be able to do surgery on your golf swing tomorrow at three o'clock."

Mark did help tremendously, but he certainly was under pressure, given my age, my physical limitations, and my success in championship play. He began to be thankful for his classes, Diplomacy 101, 201, and even 301, all of which he needed to adjust my swing from what I was positive I was doing right to a correct swing plane. He started with the left-hand grip, which was too weak. Trying to strengthen the grip, I fussed with the club, my hand, my fingers, the pad, and even Mark could not get it to fit on correctly. Then I remembered a photograph in *Golf for Women* where the LPGA teacher held a club with her right hand parallel to her hips, grasped the grip with her left hand, and then swung it around into position. All of a sudden, my left hand went where Mark wanted it.

Next, Mark discussed alignment and dropped a club on my line of flight. Immediately, like the I-don't-do-windows speech, I blurted out, "I do not do clubs that way!" Being the diplomatic teacher that he is, Mark worked through my stupid stubbornness and made my feet, hips, and, most importantly, shoulders all align parallel to the target. My shots began to improve.

Mark's big worry now was what would happen when I took all his corrections to play on the golf course. Would I play poorly and tell everyone what an incapable teacher he was and how he had messed up my game? Much to Mark's relief and my delight, I was on the mend. Lessons from a real golf professional are the answer when your swing needs help.

If you have a PGA professional at the course where you play, do not be afraid to approach him or her with questions about instruction. If you are a beginner and want to learn to play golf, look in the Yellow Pages to discover public courses where PGA professionals are available for lessons. If you feel the least bit uncomfortable or confused with your first selection, do not hesitate to make a change, but stick with a qualified teacher.

Keep It Simple

Professional teacher Peggy Kirk Bell tells the story of my missing a short putt and then asking whether I missed it to the left or to the right. My question stemmed from the fact that I was concentrating on only one thing:

keeping my head and eyes still while I was putting. (Because of that, I never saw the ball go by the hole.) This was important, because when I miss little putts my head is normally moving, or my head may be still but my eyes are sneaking a look toward the cup. Watch touring professionals when they miss short putts, and nine times out of ten it is because they peek.

Tune-Ups

While watching a crowded practice tee, Ernie Vossler, a noted teacher, remarked, "Look at all those players grooving an error."

A tune-up lesson would help most players, but they seldom rely on a teaching professional. They want to play the same clubs and ball a touring professional plays, but they ignore the fact that this professional has a famed teacher at his side. A tip of the month from a golf magazine, advice from the golf channel, a few practice balls, and off to the first tee most players go.

Golf would be an easier game if the players could see themselves. Players only see their own swings from the inside their body—their own feet, legs, hands, and arms. Meanwhile, they try to emulate swings they only see from the front.

Feel is important, but what feels perfect one day will gradually have to be exaggerated to keep the same feeling. Notice how many touring professionals have great three-week streaks and then disappear from the radar screen.

Arnold and Alice

Arnie hugs Alice after he received the Donald Ross Award from the American Society of Golf Course Architects.

Friends I have not seen for a while ask me if I am still playing golf. It has just never occurred to me to quit. At the age of seventy-five I played in two club championships, the Indiana State Amateur and the Indianapolis

Metropolitan, and I tried to qualify for my twenty-fifth appearance in the USGA Women's Senior Amateur.

I did not win, place, or even show in any of these events, but I made many new friends, forgot lots of names, hit some stupid shots, played in the rain and hundred-degree heat, and loved every minute of competing. I hit practice balls, chipped and putted, and tried all the new, hot drivers and soft-faced putters. I do not want to quit playing and competing. As long as my health cooperates, I will be swinging. I know my good friend Arnold Palmer feels the same way.

Fix Your Equipment

Occasionally I have borrowed another player's bag of clubs, and I am horrified at the contents. Layers of suntan lotion and hours in a hot car trunk have made the grips slippery and rock hard. The assortment of clubs usually contains at least one reject from a friend or relative. The side pocket of the golf bag has balls of every variety, often discolored, cut, or labeled with a bank outing—obviously found or fished from a pond. The glove is grimy, crinkled, and worn full of holes.

From the time I coveted and bought my first set of clubs, I have always carefully selected my own equipment and tried out each club. Wooden, steel, or graphite, the shaft is the most important element of a club to consider to properly fit individual requirements.

When driving a car, you adjust the seat, mirrors, and steering wheel to your needs instead of contorting your body to the previous positions. Purchasing golf equipment works in much the same way. You should adjust golf clubs to your own swing instead of trying to adjust your swing to the clubs. Most golf shops and driving ranges that sell golf equipment will let you try out a variety of clubs. A playing companion of your same ability may have a new set of clubs and will be delighted to let you experiment with a few. Proper clubs will give you better results and more enjoyment. As my father said, "They do not eat all winter." They do not have to be fed or watered, and they are only walked when you want to play.

Get your golf bag and bring it inside your home. Lay it on the couch or your bed and clean out the bag. Take a good look at your clubs. Wash your grips and rough up the surface with the saw edge of a key. Clean out the grooves of your irons. Tie your head covers together and put them back on. Consider replacing any clubs you hate, or at least take them out of the bag.

A three- or four-iron can be replaced with the new, lofted metal woods. Put rain pants and a jacket without a hood in one of the side pockets. You cannot swing wearing a hood—use a rain hat instead. Do not leave your umbrella in the trunk of your car—it does not rain there.

Check your glove and decide if you need a replacement. Your hands are the only contact you have with the club. After playing, put two or three golf balls inside your glove to hold it open to keep its shape. You will be spending four hours with this golf bag, so stock it with little extras that do not weigh much. In addition to decent golf balls, include aspirin, Band-Aids, sunscreen, tees, ball markers, and a good ball mark repair tool.

The Video

One day I decided to videotape my golf swing. Jim Ferriell, the PGA professional at the Crooked Stick Golf Club, reluctantly agreed to film me.

Once it was completed, I took the tape to his office, secured the door, and played it in the VCR. For the first thirty minutes, I looked only at my skirt, shirt, hair, shoes, and legs. I decided never to wear that outfit again, to cut my hair, and to lose thirty pounds. Then I began to critique my swing. Ugh! It looked awful to me. I was mortified that my friends and galleries had seen such a miserable swing.

I marched out, found Jim Ferriell, and said, "You need to give me many, many lessons because my swing is so dreadful that I need to start all over."

Jim looked at me and said, "Alice, remember how many times you have won with that swing?" The videotape was tossed in the trash, and that swing won many more tournaments.

Give Back to the Game

With some inspiration from Devon Brouse, director of golf, and help from Dr. Tom Templin, head of the Department of Health, Kinesiology and Leisure Studies, Pete and I started a pilot program at Purdue University for the PGA of America called Golf for Business and Life. The program is a credit physical education class taught by PGA professionals to acquaint male and female college students with the opportunities the game provides as a lifetime business tool. The pupils love the individual attention, and at the completion of the term they understand the rules and etiquette and have enough skill to play in a scramble event. Golf becomes a part of their life, and they will continue to participate in some way.

Recognizing the success of the Purdue program, the

PGA encouraged the Ryder Cup players to support the creation of similar courses at their alma maters. For the first four years, the players have designated contributions to foster Golf for Business and Life courses at these colleges:

Captain Ben Crenshaw	University of Texas–Austin
Justin Leonard	University of Texas–Austin
Davis Love III	UNC at Chapel Hill, University of Georgia
Steve Pate	UCLA, UC–Santa Barbara
Mark O'Meara	Long Beach State University
Payne Stewart	Southern Methodist University
Tom Lehman	University of Minnesota, California Polytechnic State University
Captain Curtis Strange	Wake Forest University
Mark Calcavecchia	University of Florida
David Toms	Louisiana State University
Stewart Cink	Alabama A&M University, Hampton University
Hal Sutton	Centenary College
David Duval	Georgia Tech
Jim Furyk	University of Arizona
Phil Mickelson	Arizona State University
Tiger Woods	Stanford University

Jeff Maggert	Texas A&M University
Paul Azinger	Florida State University
Scott Hoch	Wake Forest University
Scott Verplank	Oklahoma State University

Golf is a wonderful asset in business, especially for a new employee in company outings. Being able to play golf can provide many business opportunities and a lifetime of fun with friends and family. If golf has helped you in your business, given you friends, and enhanced your enjoyment of life, consider contacting the PGA of America in Palm Beach Gardens, Florida, to set up a program at your college.

The Price Is Right

Years ago, while walking in the mall with my young daughter-in-law Ann, she commented on a cute blouse in a window and how the cost, $35, was so reasonable. I considered the price outrageous, as a blouse like that used to be about $15. How was I to adjust to the inflation value of everything?

I devised a system where I divided by three, so $35 divided by three was roughly $11.50. That made the blouse a definite bargain. As the years passed with continuing inflation, my number increased from three to four and is now nearing five. I check the price, divide by five, and can relate to its value. Some common examples include:

- A car priced at $30,000 divided by 5 equals $6,000—the price is reasonable. Our 1960 car was $4,500.
- A $120,000 house divided by 5 equals $24,000—a fair price for a small house. Our first house in 1950 cost $18,000.
- A postage stamp at 37 cents divided by 5 equals 7 cents—they used to cost 3 cents. The post office leaves no choice if you want to mail a letter.
- A golf ball costing $5 divided by 5 equals $1—seems expensive. They used to be three for a dollar.
- A pair of golf shoes costing $80 divided by 5 equals $16—reasonable. They used to cost $12.
- A golf driver costing $500 divided by 5 equals $100—very expensive. They used to cost $25.
- A green fee of $250 divided by 5 equals $50—very expensive. No course used to have a fee this high.
- A green fee of $50 divided by 5 equals $10—well worth it. This was equivalent to the former fees.
- A green fee of $30 divided by 5 equals $6—a real bargain. Municipal courses used to cost $2.

Gambling vs. Score

Men enjoy mixing golf and gambling. The stakes may vary, but they are an integral part of the game, and handicaps, when used, are kept as high as possible. Games are usually match play, so the total score is irrelevant. Beating the opponent and winning some money is the object of the round.

Women approach a golf game as a personal challenge against the course. While small wagers may be made, the real object of the game is the score: the dollar won or lost dims in comparison. Great shots and miracle recoveries are all forgotten when the card is totaled and the score is too high.

Men talk about winning the match and how much money they won. Women talk about their score.

Heavy Metal

After I injured my elbows hedge trimming, a friend advised me to try a metal driver, since they had less reverberation than the wood. I could not imagine why steel would be a softer hit than wood, but plagued by remnants of tennis elbow, I would try anything.

My close friends Leslie Shannon, Robin Weiss Donnelley, and I drove to the nearby Atlantis Country Club, where the pro shop carried Taylor Made demonstration sets of drivers. Originally made for driving ranges, these metal drivers were catching on with players to use on the golf course. With great skepticism, we toted the new metal drivers to the practice range. Wow! What an impression they made! I could tell that none of the drivers had exactly the right shaft and loft for me, but knew I would immediately search for one that did.

Pete and I had just finished building the Players Club at TPC Sawgrass, Ponte Vedra, Florida, and PGA tour commissioner Deane Beman had opened the course with an impressive, creative ceremony. The elegant new pro shop was fully stocked with clubs, bags, apparel, and young assistant professionals.

Examining the selection of metal drivers displayed, I discovered the one I thought would be right for me and headed to the range with it. Trying out the new club, I noticed shot after shot went longer and the real plus—straighter. Excited, I returned to the pro shop to purchase this new metal driver. I asked the young assistant professional behind the counter what he thought of it, expecting him to rave about the great virtues of the club. Instead, this young fountain of newly acquired golf knowledge said, "Oh, Mrs. Dye, these metal drivers are no good at all. You can't hook them and you can't slice them." I immediately gave him the cash for it.

How We Lost Our Grooves

The debate regarding club and ball technology is not new. In 1948 the USGA became embroiled in a technology argument with the manufacturers regarding golf club grooves. The USGA contended that the V-shaped grooves of irons were too close together, giving more spin to the ball than was proper.

Before participating in the USGA Women's Amateur Championship at Pebble Beach, the players were required to take their clubs to USGA executive director Joe Dey to be inspected on a microscopic type of machine. If the grooves were too close together, the faces had to be ground down. Most of us had to take our clubs to the Cypress Point Golf Course golf shop, where they had a grinding machine.

To improvise, we dipped the clubs in the salt water of the Pacific Ocean so the clubfaces would become a little rougher. We believed that would provide more spin; whether it did or not, I do not know, but we thought we had outsmarted the USGA.

Some forty years later, the manufacturers did out-smart and out "legal" the USGA and the PGA Tour by forcing them to accept square grooves. These deep grooves create more spin, even from the rough. Sadly, technique is less important.

Beware of Free Clubs

Men flock to new golf equipment like it is their savior. They will spend big money for a new driver and not bat an eye. Women, however, are just the opposite. They will pay dearly for an opera ticket, hairdo, party dress, or designer purse, but when it comes to purchasing new golf equipment or a ticket to a golf tournament, they shy away. Women ask their male counterparts to give them new putters, wedges, or clubs for birthdays or Christmas. Why would anyone want a new club at Christmas unless they live in a warm climate? The time to buy one is when you are playing and can try it out. Do not take a hand-me-down club from someone much bigger and stronger than you are. The shaft will be too stiff.

Do not wait for a gift; you may be stuck with it. For years, Dale Morey, an accomplished amateur and one of the game's best putters, used an old battered blade putter that he loved and stroked with great success. When he married, his new bride noticed that while he had new clubs, his putter was quite shabby. Not being a golfer or knowledgeable about the game, she decided to delight him with a new putter and bought the shiniest gold one she could find. Their marriage lasted a lifetime, but this definitely was a shaky start!

Car Keys—Where Are They?

Golf is fun. It is social, good exercise, and competitive, so prepare for your game. Get organized and give yourself time to get into a good rhythm. Think ahead about where you left your clubs, shoes, hat, and car keys. Allow some extra time to get to the golf course to hit practice balls, putt, or at least take some warm-up swings. Count the hour before you play as part of your game. Your mind and body need a little extra time to put the brakes on the fast track of your life.

When you hit a poor shot, get over it fast and start thinking about the next shot and how you are going to hit a great recovery. Do not dwell on a miss-hit, but love the challenge of the next shot. Stay positive. Just how poorly would you have to play to wish you were back at the office working or home housecleaning?

Tommy Armour

Tommy Armour tells the story of a wager he made with a friend. They were watching two famous professionals playing an important match, concluding on the eighteenth hole of the Winged Foot Golf Club. The loser missed a two-foot putt, and Tommy's friend exclaimed, "Even I could have made that putt!"

Tommy bet his friend $100 he could not make the same putt, and the man, eager to stroke the putt in and collect, agreed. Tommy said, "Not right now—after lunch."

During the meal, Tommy related stories of famous missed putts, bumpy greens, grain, and green speed, building up the pressure. By the time his friend was allowed to try the putt, he never even hit the hole.

As pressure builds for me when I am facing a difficult shot to a green surrounded by trouble, I visualize the perfect shot, carefully aim the club and my body, and then mentally put myself back on the practice tee with this club hitting a perfect shot. The bunkers, water, or any other trouble disappear, and my practice tee swing can take over.

Pete says I am a "bell ringer," meaning that when the tournament begins, my game responds. For me, pressure starts to build even before an event. I can feel it begin to envelop me and start to turn my focus to the tournament play. I mentally discard other distractions and know that pressure can help me if I work it into my routine. My body begins to recognize this feeling, and digestive juices slow. I have to eat simple foods, cut caffeine, and monitor sugar. I know the adrenaline is building, and I begin to slow down a bit and work rhythm and balance into my practice warm-up.

Once I am on the course, I know I will be stronger and must allow for this sudden strength. As pressure builds throughout the round, I try to use it to my advantage. I work on blocking out distractions, focusing on the next shot, and keep thinking of rhythm and balance. The key for me is to maintain control and stay within the moment. I do not allow myself to look back at a missed shot or ahead to possible victory or defeat. The more pressure I feel, the more adrenaline and additional strength I have. Knowing this, I allow for longer drives and take less club for shots to the green. I think distance, not line, on long putts and hold my head and eyes still on short ones. Enjoy the pressure. It can work for you.

Intimidation

Often in social events I am paired with a high handicapper. Since I am an accomplished player, it is evident they are scared, very nervous, sometimes even on the verge of panic, or, even worse, hung over from a night of drowning their dread. Recalling my fright in the early days when I played an exhibition with Babe Zaharias or

Alice and Byron Nelson at the PGA Champions
Dinner in 2000.

Byron Nelson, I remember how gracious, calming, and encouraging they were. Now it is my job to help my high handicapper become comfortable.

One day I was paired with a lady who told me how scared she was to play a round with me and that all her friends would be waiting behind the eighteenth green to console her with drinks and lunch in the clubhouse. With some easy conversation and encouragement from me, she relaxed and was playing well for her level of skill. As we walked off the seventeenth green, she told me her fears were unfounded and it had been a joy to play with me. Thankfully, I had been able to calm her fears, just as Babe and Byron had done for me so many years earlier.

Moments later she stepped in a hole, turned her ankle, and fell to the ground. She managed to get up but was now completely disheveled: grass stains on her skirt, visor bent, hair cascading out of her bun, knees skinned, and a trickle of blood running down her shin. As she hobbled up the eighteenth fairway toward the green, I knew her friends would think that playing with me had demolished her.

Pulling herself together, she explained her condition to her friends at the green and said that playing with me had really been fun. Thank goodness I was not the reason she needed the drinks they had brought to console her.

Losing Is No Fun

Some people are afraid of losing. One very good player I knew would advance to the final match of a championship, and the night before the match, she would pretend to drink too much so she had the excuse of being hung over should she not win.

Nobody rises to the occasion every time, and it is hard when you fail. It is difficult to have others watch you fall short, especially when it is your family or close friends. They do not think you have failed; they are proud of you because you tried. When anyone dubs a shot or misses a crucial putt, it hurts, but no one is always on his or her game.

I still remember a championship match nearly sixty years ago where I faced an eight-foot downhill putt to extend the match to extra holes. Even today I can recall looking at the line, stroking the putt, and watching in disbelief as it came up an inch short. It is still a bad memory. We all come up short sometimes, but we cannot be too tough on ourselves. The real failure is not trying.

When you choose to compete, you expose yourself to failure as well as praise. You win sometimes but lose many more times. It is not easy to have others see your poor shots and missed putts. Victories are very rewarding, but even Tiger Woods has lost more times than he has won.

I have won about fifty tournaments, but at least five hundred times I have lost and had to shake hands with a smile and maintain a gracious composure. It was hard, really hard, especially when I had played poorly. Life gives everyone some failures, and golf competitions have helped me handle many of them. Admittedly there have been times when I did not deal with losing very well, but being a gracious loser is every bit as important as being a humble winner.

On Course with Nancy Lopez

I first met Nancy Lopez at the Women's Western Golf Tournament. She was wandering around the grounds of the Flossmoor Country Club, just south of Chicago, where we were playing practice rounds for the event. I asked if I could help her, and Nancy said she was hunting for the practice range. The club did not have one, but the Western had made arrangements for the contestants to use one a few blocks away.

I offered Nancy a ride, and together we drove to the nearby practice range. She joined some other young players and made arrangements to return to the club after her practice, so she did not need me to give her a ride back. In that short time together, Nancy impressed me with her sparkle, her composure, and her friendliness.

The following year I came to compete in the Women's Western tournament at the Blue Hills Country Club in Kansas City. After qualifying, I noted that I had drawn Nancy for my first match. She was fifteen and I was forty-five, exactly three times her age.

This time I did not have a car, and I asked Nancy for a ride. She had been driving for a year, since her home state of New Mexico permitted driver's licenses at age fourteen. I joined her in a bright red convertible with the top down. We took off full speed ahead.

On the way to the course, we stopped to see Nancy's parents, Domingo and Marina Lopez. I could see the love they poured out to Nancy and her returning affection and respect for them. Leaving with hugs, kisses, and good-luck wishes, we hit the road again at full speed.

After a warm-up session on the practice range, we began our match, with Domingo discreetly watching. I was still at the top of my game, and Nancy was already impressive even at her young age. We seesawed back and forth, winning and losing holes until the eighteenth, where Nancy prevailed. My congratulating handshake was the beginning of lengthy admiration for the talent, sportsmanship, and graciousness of Nancy Lopez.

After the match, Domingo walked up and said, "Thank you, Mrs. Dye. You are the first player who has treated Nancy as a fellow competitor instead of just some young bratty kid."

Nancy continued her winning ways before losing in the finals to Debbie Massey. A few years later she reached the finals of the Women's Western at the Country Club of Colorado and won the championship.

The love that Nancy's family bestowed on her flowed from her to all her fans throughout her career. To watch Nancy play is to be drawn into her joy of competition.

Nancy and I played in several more amateur tournaments together before I began competing in senior events and she began her LPGA career. We are long-distance friends but bound together as members of the family of golf. We care about each other, and I did not hesitate to ask her to write the foreword for this book. She readily accepted.

Nancy Lopez became not only a great player but also one of golf's finest ambassadors. Her personality, vitality, talent, and smile caused the British to call her "Nancy with the laughing eyes." She is an inspiration, a leader, and a true spirit of the game. She has improved the world's perception of women's golf.

Calling Rules

In all the tournaments I have played, I have never called a rule on any other player. In stroke play, if I see a fellow competitor about to do something wrong, I always stop her. It is my obligation to protect the field. If it is match play, I trust my opponent is not breaking a rule intentionally, so I wait and explain the rule after the match. Players who use rules to win matches are not popular with other players.

Keep Up

Notoriously slow players don't realize what torture they provide for their playing companions and the groups behind them.

One gentleman I knew was overly deliberate, rarely organized when it was his turn to hit, and tiresome on the green. We were playing behind him one afternoon, and his group was holding us up, as well as everyone else behind us. Our fifteenth green was quite near the sixteenth tee where he was considering hitting his drive. After he finally teed off, I walked over and mentioned that his foursome had the whole course stacked up. He looked puzzled and said, "That's impossible. There is no one in front of us."

Remember: It is not the group behind you that you need to watch. It is the group in front of you that you need to keep up with.

Have an Attitude

When Jack Nicklaus began a round with bogies, he always kept a positive attitude. He said golf is a game of good and bad shots, and he looked forward to the good ones because he had already hit the bad ones.

Ben Hogan once said he averaged only seven good shots a round.

Sports psychologists work with players to keep their attitude positive. They preach that poor shots are not punishment for off-course behavior. Recovery shots are what golf is all about.

My good friend amateur champion Carol Semple Thompson, winner of every major amateur championship and a twelve-time-and-counting Curtis Cup player, says that when she was growing up, she got so upset during a round that it scared her. She told me, "When I was sixteen, I was playing so badly that on the back nine I got so mad that I actually saw red. Everything took on a red aura, and it was very scary. It made me wonder how I could get so mad." Carol admitted that the incident changed her perspective on the game. She said, "I was determined, at that point, to never let the game get to me that badly again. And it hasn't. I have always been able to keep my emotions under wraps."

Using mental practice tapes has helped Carol. They include relaxing techniques such as the feeling of going down in an elevator and visual tapes where the night before a competition she plays all eighteen holes, each shot hit rhythmically with perfect results. She sees the drive landing in the middle of the fairway and the next shot bouncing on the green and rolling toward the pin. Carol also practices counting backward from five to zero and feels the nervousness drain out as she reaches zero. Practicing this takes mental discipline but can easily become a habit to use when pressure builds and you need to keep a positive attitude.

Mystery Strokes

Why are the little black dots a tournament committee writes on the scorecard to note the handicap strokes always on the longest holes instead of the hardest par fours? Handicap strokes are given to try to equalize the ability of players. The most difficult par three or par four for a low-handicap player to par may be an easy bogey for the high handicapper, who would have the advantage should they both bogey.

The *USGA Handicap Manual* states, "Difficulty in making par is not necessarily the need of a stroke—rather it should be on a hole where it is most likely to be needed by the higher-handicapped player to obtain a half in a match. Generally the longer the hole, the greater the need for the higher handicapped player to receive a stroke."

Low handicappers believe strokes should be on par fours that are difficult for them. Instead they should think about where they would most want to have to *give* an opponent a stroke. Thinking of giving rather than receiving strokes makes sense of the allocation of the first strokes on the longest par-five holes—usually the easiest for a low handicapper and the most difficult for the higher handicapper.

Good Sportsmanship

How does a player learn, or an instructor teach, good sportsmanship? It is the very soul of golf. You are your own scorekeeper and referee to call even unintentional infractions. There are no teammates to share the blame.

The spirit of good sportsmanship is passed from experienced players, parents, and coaches to beginners. Methods vary. Charlie Nicklaus, Jack's father, once took the rest of Jack's clubs back to his closet after Jack lofted a club into a tree. I recall gallerying a match where a young player lost on the sixth extra hole. He began pounding his club and gyrating around in frustration. The gallery was heading back to the clubhouse for the trophy presentation. I knew this young player was misbehaving and would damage his reputation if he did not pull himself together. I walked over to him and said, "You have between here and the clubhouse to learn good sportsmanship." It was a long walk for him, but he gathered himself and came in smiling. He won many future matches, eventually becoming a college golf coach. He taught good sportsmanship.

At the Genuity Championship played on the famous Doral "Blue Monster," Tiger Woods missed a very makeable putt for birdie on one of the finishing holes. As he walked away, a spike on his left shoe caught a bit of turf. Despite being upset over missing the birdie putt, one that lessened his chance of winning, Tiger stopped, walked back toward the hole, and smoothed the surface of the green with his putter. In the NBC booth, golf analyst Johnny Miller said, "Only in golf would you help players that you are trying to beat. If it was football, the player would be dragging his cleats." Johnny's comment symbolizes the spirit of sportsmanship in golf.

Tiger Woods and Alice at the PGA Champions Dinner in 2002.

Jack Nicklaus

Pete and I had completed several golf courses before we considered studying the great lore of golf course architecture in books. We had gathered some books but gave them little attention. We did, however, decide to visit Scotland in 1963 to study the famous courses and learn firsthand from the architects of old.

We played, photographed, and memorized the contouring fairway swales, wooden sleepers, green shapes, small tees, pot bunkers, and open green approaches. Pete held the camera while I slid down every deep bunker to give depth perspective to the photos. He claimed my red hat and sweater gave better contrast than his navy Windbreaker, so I got a firsthand view of the bottom of every Scottish bunker. We arrived home, excited and enthusiastic, ready to create the Crooked Stick Golf Club in Carmel, Indiana, and to design and build The Golf Club just outside Columbus, Ohio, home of Jack Nicklaus.

Pete had competed with Jack in numerous events while Jack was still an amateur and now admired his professional career. He invited Jack to visit the construction site of The Golf Club and critique the various holes. Jack was twenty-seven years old, and at that time thirty was considered old in any sport, so Jack was considering other career options. He walked the dirt fairways and hit shots to the greens, suggested some tiered bulking, proposed many ideas, and fell in love with golf course design.

When Charles Fraser told Jack he was going to build another course on Hilton Head Island, Jack recommended Pete and agreed to collaborate with him. Working together, Pete and Jack created a new style of architecture. When the course opened and Arnold Palmer won the initial PGA Tour Heritage Tournament at Harbour Town, national publicity established the budding architectural careers of Alice and Pete Dye and Jack Nicklaus. Several of our other joint ventures petered out, as Jack's game did not fade but only improved. He continued to win tournaments, including twenty major championships, and successfully combined his golf prowess with designing out-

Longtime friend Jack Nicklaus with Alice and Pete at the ASGCA annual meeting.

standing courses all over the world. We treasure the life-long friendship we have with Barbara and Jack.

I continued to compete in amateur tournaments, but Pete stored his clubs and devoted his time and full attention to designing golf courses and hands-on construction.

Half a Portrait

Harbour Town Golf Links was officially opened by the play of the Heritage Classic Tournament in November 1968. Pete, Jack Nicklaus, and I had collaborated to design and build this revolutionary golf course featuring small target greens, railroad ties, and waste bunkers.

During the construction, while Pete was busy directing the shaping of the twelfth hole, he sent me ahead to begin work on the thirteenth. I designed a heart-shaped green protected by a large sand bunker and shored the front with cypress planks. When Pete refurbished the course thirty years later, all his bulkheading had decayed; my cypress planks were the only wooden features that had not rotted.

For the wall of the clubhouse grillroom, famous artist Colby Whitmore had been commissioned to paint a portrait of Pete and Jack standing together with the landmark red-and-white lighthouse in the background. Pete's parents, Pink and Elizabeth, attended the opening of the course. When Mr. Whitmore approached their table and introduced himself, Elizabeth told him that while her husband had come to see the new golf course, she had come to see the portrait, and she loved it. Mr. Whitmore, pleased that she admired his work, said that he had something special to show her; he would dash to his studio and be right back.

Pink panicked, knowing the astronomical price of Whitmore's paintings and the prospect that he would be expected to purchase one of them. Shortly, the artist returned holding a small scroll. Standing beside Elizabeth, he held his hand aloft, and the narrow scroll unwound, revealing a portrait of Pete standing alone. Mr. Whitmore said he had torn Jack's half away because Jack had lost so much weight that he had to start a new portrait, and he would be delighted to give the original of Pete's half to her. Elizabeth was overjoyed but not nearly as much as Pink, who was relieved he would not have to pay for it.

Today the painting of Pete and a slimmed-down Jack hangs in the Harbour Town Golf Links clubhouse along with portraits of all the winners of the Heritage Classic Tournament. I have the narrow portrait of Pete alone in our home.

"Pete's half" of Mr. Whitmore's
portrait of Pete and Jack Nicklaus.

The Trailer

The summer we were building The Golf Club in Ohio, Pete thought it would be great if he bought a trailer. He wanted to move it on-site so the boys and I could live there. I had been on construction sites and knew they were dusty or muddy, desolate areas. Trailer life did not appeal to me at all. How was I going to get out of the situation?

One Sunday morning after a Saturday night of much

gaiety, where Pete had been the life of the party, I was inspired. Knowing he felt lousy, but would certainly not admit it, I suggested we go look at trailers.

The weather was sunny and hot, and the temperature was climbing toward triple digits as we drove to the edge of town to the trailer sales lot. Even the salesman was per-spiring as he began to show us a two-bedroom trailer perched on cement blocks. The sun had baked it, so when he opened the door, it was like an inferno.

We climbed up the rickety steps, and I began to admire all the tiny spaces, including the cubbyhole shower, the undersize double bed, the narrow bunks for the boys, and the minuscule kitchen. The trailer was rocking on its blocks, and the temperature was at least 110 degrees inside. I looked over and saw Pete turning green, longing for the cool luxuries of our own home. It was the end of trailer life.

He Said—She Said

Two professors from Emory University once requested an appointment to discuss our husband-wife part-nership. They were interviewing couples who had worked together for many years on various projects. They asked who made the inspirational artistic designs and who made the practical ones. The professors were surprised when I told them that all of our innovative designs have come from Pete's creative imagination. He was the artist, the sculptor, the visionary. He wanted the mounding profiles to blend into the background, the sand to show, the rough to contrast, the vistas to be long, the shapes of the holes to vary, the greens with depth and at ground level, the lines sharp, clean, and smooth, and the tee angles to determine the degree of difficulty.

Some of our design ideas, such as wisps of pampas grass, bulkheading, waste bunkers, and island greens, have been imitated many times by other architects. My collaboration was always more practical, based on playability. I was always thinking of the player and what was going to happen to a golf shot. I considered how the high-handicap man or woman was going to play the hole, whether the uphill climbs were too steep, the downhills too sloped, and the bunker entrances too abrupt. While I did not spend the long hours on-site that Pete did, I always came often enough to offer approval or new ideas.

I did become very concerned as I watched various foursomes of women playing courses where the holes were too long, so we began incorporating shorter yardage into our courses. Soon I was in demand to add forward tees to existing courses, but the traveling was interfering with my work with Pete, so I made a chart and video to help other architects design or add forward tees.

Pete does not have an office full of plans for greens, so each one he builds is an original, created on-site. Sometimes I think his greens look too similar, too difficult, too flat, too narrow, or are too offset, and I discuss it with him. I know he hates it, but he listens.

Pete and I do confer about strategy, driving distances, types of turf, color of sand, and the playability of our courses. We try hard to devise holes that will challenge the long hitter and still be manageable for those of less strength. No longer do we reward the long carry with the easier shot to the green. We do not believe the long hitter should have an easy short iron to an open green and the shorter hitter a difficult long iron shot over a bunker. Many famous old holes feature this strategy, but whenever possible, we reverse it.

The Hole Golfers Love to Hate

In 1980 PGA Tour Commissioner Deane Beman telephoned Pete and asked him to build a championship golf course to host the Player's Championship. Deane wanted it to be the fifth major, alongside the Masters, the USGA Open, the British Open, and the PGA Championship. The location was the area of Jacksonville Beach, Florida.

*Celebration at the famous par-three island
seventeenth green at the TPC course in
Florida during the Players Championship.*

Deane and Pete considered several sites, but the
Fletcher brothers made them an offer they could not
refuse. The land was swampy and dense with vegetation,
but the price was right. Later Pete wrote, "My only compatriots in the impenetrable jungle were deer, alligators,
wild boar, and deadly snakes."

Pete devised a moat system, gradually drained the
land, and began construction. Deane wanted spectator
mounds, but he never envisioned the huge piles of excess
muck Pete fashioned into gigantic gallery mounds.

There are many PGA Tour—owned courses now, but
this was the first, and the budget was low. Sand was at a
premium, but Pete discovered a large deposit near the
par-three seventeenth-green site. As he kept digging and
hauling the sand to other green locations around the

course, the ground around the seventeenth-green site vanished. One day, while staring at the huge hole in the earth, Pete asked me what I thought of filling it with water. I replied, "Why not keep digging and make an island green?"

With those words, the seventeenth-hole island green was born. Pete then contoured the green with the back third sloping toward the water. I teased him, saying, "Pete, I can just see the telecast of the first tournament. The coverage begins and then the announcer says, 'Ladies and gentlemen, unfortunately the first threesome is still standing on the seventeenth tee. There is a strong following wind, and no balls have been able to stay on the green.'"

Pete laughed and positioned a small bunker at the front and sloped the rear of the green back toward the tee. During the PGA Tour Championship, the drama builds for the professionals and spectators as the leaders near the seventeenth hole. It is heart-stopping for the players, who breathe a big sigh of relief once their ball is on the green.

During practice rounds of the tournament, the players all allow their caddies to attempt a shot to the green. Few succeed. Each year the ground crew retrieves 200,000 balls from the pond. Every few years they must haul out the large pile of divots that fly into the water in front of the tee.

Players teeing off the first hole know that ultimately they have to play the seventeenth-hole island green, and the pressure builds as the round progresses. It is a fun hole except when you are competing for a championship. During final rounds, Seve Ballesteros recorded a nine, Greg Norman a seven, and Payne Stewart and Len Mattice eights. Joey Sindelar once made an ace in the second round and a seven on Sunday. No wonder NBC's Gary Koch called the seventeenth "the toughest 132 yards of real estate in golf."

Did I ever dream that the seventeenth at the TPC Stadium Course in Jacksonville would become such a famous hole? Certainly not fifty years earlier when I began my love affair with the game of golf.

Diplomas

The world can take everything away from you—money, health, and friends—but it cannot take away your education. From kindergarten on, it is the foundation of your life.

World War II interrupted Pete's high school days at Asheville School in Asheville, North Carolina. Then he went to work for Northwestern Mutual Insurance Company before he had a chance to graduate from Rollins

College. His regret that he did not have a high school or college diploma lingered with him over the years.

In 1996, when Purdue University needed to revamp their North Course, Pete pitched in and offered to help raise the money and build an entirely new course with the help of the agronomy students. When construction began and the students showed up, he was horrified at the modern-day ponytails and earrings, but they all turned out to be dedicated hard workers.

At the opening-day ceremony for the golf course, a grateful Purdue staff surprised Pete by naming the clubhouse after him. On the way home, he leaned over to me and whispered, "Alice, I do not need another [bleeping] house. What I need is a diploma!"

The word spread, and the following spring at the graduation ceremony, Purdue University awarded Pete an honorary doctorate in agronomy. Dr. Pete Dye finally had a diploma. A few years later, and more than fifty years after leaving Asheville School, Pete was honored with their highest alumni award of merit. As a special surprise, Asheville School's president presented him with the long-desired high school diploma, dated 1944.

Some people may not appreciate the value of a diploma, but when you do not have one, you know it. I was fortunate to graduate from Rollins College and complete an education that gave me knowledge but most of all confidence. College golf not only improved my game but also

introduced me to my best longtime friends, Lee Hilkene and Pete Dye.

Recently, in recognition of my achievements, I was awarded an honorary doctorate degree during an impressive graduation ceremony at Rollins College. I was seated on the front part of the stage, with the faculty on the bleachers behind me. Facing me from below the stage were approximately 700 graduates, their families, and my own family. Rick Goings, CEO of Tupperware, read the citation. When he came to the part about my being the first woman member of the American Society of Golf Course Architects and the first woman board member of the PGA of America, he broke from the script and said, "In other words, she broke up the 'old boy's club.'" Everyone—students, parents, and faculty—broke into applause. We are now Dr. Alice and Dr. Pete.

The Spouse

In recent years, Pete has suddenly become "the spouse," a role he plays to the hilt. On the opening day of the First Tee Program, which teaches golf and life skills to inner-city youth, held in New York City's Central Park, I was in attendance as president of the American Society of

*Pete and President George Bush relax at the
Whistling Straits course in Wisconsin.*

Golf Course Architects. Pete accompanied me, and while
chatting with the honorary chairman, President George
H. Bush, at times upstaged by his wife, Barbara, Pete said
to the president, "I am here as a spouse." President Bush
answered, "I am very familiar with that role."

When I was invited to serve on the PGA of America
Board of Directors, Pete again became the spouse. The
PGA traditionally hosts a Champions Dinner the Tues-
day preceding the championship for past winners. The
defending champion selects the menu. Past presidents
and present board members of the PGA are invited.

I offered to dine with the wives, but PGA of America
chief executive officer Jim Awtrey said I was a board
member, not a *woman* board member, and should be
seated as such. I told Pete I would be the only woman at
the dinner. He said, "Of course. No woman has ever won

the PGA Championship or been PGA president, and you are the only woman PGA board member."

My table included the great gentleman of golf Byron Nelson. We were situated near the table where Jack Nicklaus and Tiger Woods were seated. We could overhear Tiger, in answer to his query, tell Jack how he played each hole at St. Andrews, in Scotland, to win the British Open. As Tiger related where each of his drives landed, Jack knew exactly what bunkers he had carried and what kind of shot he had remaining. Meanwhile Pete, being the good sport that he is, was in another dining room, seated with Mrs. Byron Nelson, Barbara Nicklaus, and the other spouses.

It is customary for the defending champion to select a gift for his dinner guests. His wife or girlfriend selects a gift for the spouses. Pete had a great time with all the wives, but his gift was a Waterford cut-glass vanity set—a tray holding cosmetic jars, perfume bottles, and powder brushes.

Pete jokingly complained so much about his gift that I promised I would give him the handsome clock I knew Tiger had selected for his dinner guests. When Tiger's gift box arrived at our home, Pete eagerly unpacked it. He was delighted with the handsome wooden panel encasing four clock faces, each one featuring the time in the zone where Tiger had won his four majors: St. Andrews, Scotland;

Augusta, Georgia; Chicago, Illinois; and Pebble Beach, California.

Suddenly, Pete put the clock down and pouted. He said, "Just look at this inscription. It says, 'Presented to Alice Dye from Tiger Woods.'"

He Calls Me Ally

Yes, Pete did sneak a baby raccoon onto an airplane. Yes, he was responsible for causing a bit of a ruckus on a transatlantic flight when he opened a travel bag containing an overripe banana and a swarm of gnats escaped into the cabin. Yes, he once nearly destroyed a Jacuzzi in a Palm Springs hotel when the sand in the pockets of his work pants, which he was attempting to wash *while sitting in the Jacuzzi,* clogged up the drain.

Yes, he does love Motel 6 instead of fancy hotels. Yes, his favorite breakfast meal is an unusual combination of Fiber One, Quaker Oats, figs, bananas, red grapes, and prunes topped with yogurt and red raspberry jam. And yes, he calls me Ally.

"Pink's" Dynasty

The Dye legacy of golf course design started at the Mount Vernon Inn in Pennsylvania on old Route U.S. 40 when Pete's father, Paul "Pink" Dye, driving home to Urbana, Ohio, stopped and hit his first bucket of golf balls. Enchanted with the game, when he returned home he began playing but had to travel to nearby towns to find a golf course. His wife, Elizabeth's family owned land on the outskirts of Urbana, and he finally persuaded them to allow him to build nine holes on the most rolling portions, which were least suitable for farming.

On this nine-hole course, called the Urbana Country Club, Pete learned the game and some greenskeeping experience. Seventy years later, our son P. B. Dye returned to build a beautiful additional nine holes and a log cabin summer home on one of his new fairways. Every year, to honor his grandparents, P. B. and his lovely wife, Jeannie, host a Dye Memorial Skins Tournament and fabulous yard party and bonfire. Their friends from school, work, and golf come from near and far to gather for great fun and golf with rather lenient rules. Somewhere grandparents Pink and Elizabeth are smiling.

Pink's dynasty continues with all the young men who have worked with Pete and me and learned from us. Our two sons, Perry and P. B., Pete's brother Roy, and Roy's sons and one daughter head the list. Other young men we have had the privilege of inaugurating in the architectural profession include:

Bill Coore	Chris Lutzke	Scott Pool
Brian Curley	Jason McCoy	Lee Schmidt
Tom Doak	Greg Muirhead	Keith Sparkman
John Harbottle	William Newcomb	Bobby Weed
Mike Langkau	Michael O'Connor	Rod Whitman
Tim Liddy	David Pfaff	

Golf professionals Jack Nicklaus and Greg Norman augmented their architectural careers in collaboration with us. From one bucket of balls came this dynasty of creation.

Unroll the Hole

Clients call Pete and me to build a golf course on what they consider to be perfectly beautiful land. It may be rolling, wooded, on a hillside, or contain winding streams.

None of these features may fit with eighteen holes, but it is our job to pick the best sites for as many holes as possible and work in the rest. After routing maps and the permitting process have been completed, construction begins. First, all environmental areas are protected by bright orange fencing. Then the trailers, bulldozers, well drillers, pipes, and lake liners arrive at the site. The pristine property is stripped of topsoil, which is stored in piles so fairways can be shaped and irrigated. Most of the stately old trees are saved, but some must be cut down.

Watching the construction process makes a landowner heartsick. He expected the golf holes just to be unrolled and laid down like a giant roll of sod. It is months and sometimes years before the last bulldozer leaves, the trailers hauled away, and his dream materializes. Now his land is more beautiful than ever and enjoyed by all who play there.

The Dye Conglomerate

The Pete Dye Inc. "firm" is really a figment of people's imagination. We are a mom-and-pop partnership held together first by Charlotte McNamara and now by two assistants, Diane Darsch and Shannon Meeks.

Charlotte ran Pete's first design office in Carmel, a suburb of Indianapolis, by herself. Pete was traveling a great deal to various job sites, and often the small Indianapolis airport was weathered in, and he could not return home. In 1970 we moved to Delray Beach, Florida, where one of the three airports—Miami, Fort Lauderdale, or West Palm Beach—would always be open. Diane Darsch, affectionately known to us as "Dinky," has for many years been our dedicated secretary, file clerk, errand girl, and good friend. Pete sketches his golf course routings on the dining room table. Topographic maps litter the rug. Sixty begs for a walk.

During the summers we used to visit Indianapolis and stay at my brother, Perry O'Neal's home on the fourteenth hole of Crooked Stick. In 1991 we built our new summer home on the eighteenth hole of Crooked Stick. Pete Dye Inc. went in a suitcase to Carmel, Indiana, and Shannon Meeks became "manpower," running our computer, assisting with office tasks, and becoming a special friend to us. On the dining room table Pete and architect Tim Liddy draw their routings, while Sixty lies at their feet. I give them sandwiches and suggestions.

In the midst of a recession in the golf course design business, a leading golf magazine contacted Pete Dye Inc. about the slowdown. They wanted to know how many people we had let go from our firm. Pete, with his quick wit, replied that the only way he could reduce the size of his firm would be to get a divorce.

Hello

Clients who telephone our home office expect to hear one of those prerecorded messages with eight different options or at least a secretary to take the call. That is not our style. We answer the telephone when we are home and ask people to leave a message on our answering machine when we are not.

For many years, when Pete and I were traveling, we put call forwarding on to the home of Pete's mother, Elizabeth. Ninety-four years young, she sat in her living room and kept a list of the telephone messages in a notebook on her tray table. She would answer the call of some flamboyant developer who said he had great land and good financing, decide she did not like him, and cross him off the list. Then a moneyless fellow churchgoer (she always checked this out) would call from some rocky wilderness location in need of a course designer. She would feel sorry for him and say, "I'm sure Pete will be interested."

If Pete's mother was playing bridge, the caller had no chance. No one was given priority, including the chairman of the board of the ITT Sheraton company. He was greeted with "Pete is just too busy" before she hung up the telephone and resumed her card game.

One caller intrigued her until he started pestering

her about Pete's fee. She artfully dodged his questions, but he persisted and said he had read about a low fee in a magazine. She countered, "It must have been an *old* magazine."

Elizabeth would take the telephone, tablet, and her glasses to her bathroom dressing table when she took her morning shower. While drying off one day, she heard the telephone ring and answered cheerfully, "The Dyes," a greeting that would cover her residence as well as ours.

On the line, Elizabeth heard a distinctive English accent asking for architect "Pater" Dye. She could just visualize the gentleman behind the voice sitting at a huge desk in a paneled office, suited in a tweed jacket complete with ascot. While he prattled on about arranging a call back, Elizabeth glanced at the mirror and mused, "I wonder if he knows he is talking to a naked ninety-four-year-old lady."

Sixty—Winner of the Dog Lottery

While Pete and I were living in the Dominican Republic, building the Teeth of the Dog course, I decided we needed a watchdog. Our last dog had been a handsome white German shepherd, but knowing the protective temperament of shepherds, I thought a mixed breed would be a better idea.

I searched the classified ads in the newspaper and found German shepherd—mix puppies for sale. Pete and I drove to the rugged neighborhood that was listed in the advertisement.

We parked in front of a small house surrounded by a heavy chain-link fence with a "Beware of Dog" sign hanging on it. The lady owner opened the gate, and we walked inside. Pete was worried about the hubcaps on the car.

Inside the tiny living room was a box of five puppies. I picked up the cutest one and said we would take her.

Pete, still worried about the car, asked, "How much?" The woman said she hated to charge us, but she needed the money to buy food for the remaining puppies. The price was $20, and Pete paid her. As we were leaving, she offered him a little ribbon collar that he accepted. He gave her another $20.

Just as we reached our car, the woman ran out of her house and showed us a flimsy three-foot chain for a leash. She asked if we would like it. Pete donated another $20, and we started home with the hubcaps still on and me holding the little six-week-old puppy.

"What should we call her?" I asked. Pete said, "Let's see, twenty dollars plus twenty dollars plus twenty dollars is sixty. Let's call her Sixty."

Two years later, Sixty suddenly died of a liver ailment. Pete was so upset I knew we should get a new puppy right away.

The *Indianapolis Star* listed German shepherd puppies for sale at a kennel south of town. We chose the last of the litter, a six-month-old all-black beauty, begging for Pete's attention. It was love at first sight. She became Sixty II.

Whenever Pete travels by private plane, his loyal friend Sixty is a passenger. She accompanies him so often that many times air traffic controllers will ask, "Is Sixty aboard?"

Sixty has become jet-savvy. She sits facing the front as the airplane ascends and then jumps to a seat facing the rear as the airplane descends. When there is catered food, it always includes dog treats.

German shepard Sixty Dye, Pete's best friend.

Design Evolution

A book on our design philosophy would have to be revised daily, as Pete and I have tried to design each new golf course to keep up with the times. When we first began building courses, fairway watering systems had just started to take away the roll and change the game from one played on the ground to one played in the air. Holes suddenly were playing much longer.

Dean Knuth, formerly with the United States Golf Association and the originator of its present handicap system, noted that in the 1920s Bobby Jones used to carry the ball two hundred yards, and it would roll another hundred yards. One-third of his distance was the roll on the ground.

Watered fairways drastically reduced the roll and changed golf from a sport of ladies and gentlemen who hit it "short and straight," into a game of strength à la Jack Nicklaus and Tiger Woods. As the game changes, Pete and I keep adapting our courses to the new irrigation, new turf grasses, new clubs, and, especially, the new golf balls.

The architects of old had different philosophies, but most of them rewarded the long hitter. Pete and I were two scratch handicappers in our late twenties when we began our first design. Young, strong, and full of ideas, we designed courses to match our ability. We featured forced carries, deep bunkers, wide undulating fairways, abrupt bulkheading, wild rough grasses for definition, and wood, wood, wood. We used telephone poles, planks, and railroad ties to shore bunkers or form retaining walls. We were even accused of building the only courses that could burn down.

Our greens were small and tightly bunkered, or large multicontoured ones, sometimes with water or a ravine on one side. They were designed on-site, as we had no set of hole or green plans. Pete's creative ideas sculpted the land. He built golf courses for the love of it, with no concern for reward. He just wanted to be there and build a great golf course. He did not even have routing plans and sometimes strayed off the owner's property. He walked the land, finding every natural green site and saving every important tree. His only measuring device was his stride—110 steps for each 100 yards.

Although I continued competing, Pete's tournament golf came to a halt, since he was on-site every day, including weekends. He always considered Sunday a good day for construction.

I would often accompany Pete and walk the site, make suggestions, shake my head, and raise my eyebrows in disbelief at some of his ideas, but I never ever had his creative imagination. He always listened to my suggestions and many times would incorporate my ideas, embellished by his creativity. Pete never saw a hole unfinished. I would be looking at woods, underbrush, ditches, and mud, but Pete was envisioning a hole with grass, bunkers, and a green. He always saw the hole completely finished, probably even with a flagstick.

Fired

Early in our architectural career, Pete and I had to provide a potential golf course owner with a map drawn to scale. The client was TRW, based in Cleveland, Ohio. At the time, they were working on the module that would soon land on the moon.

Pete carefully drew thirty-six holes to scale on a small sketchpad. He then asked me to enlarge it on a sheet of paper about forty inches square. It barely fit on our kitchen table. I had to draw with India ink and two active sons jiggling the table.

I expanded the holes, drew in the bunkers, trees, and lakes, and then copied the scale. I thought I had done a marvelous job, and Pete took the plan to Mr. Wright, chief executive officer of TRW. Impressed with the layout, he gave it to his engineers to consider.

Almost immediately, one of the engineers returned and said, "Mr. Wright, I did not know we owned land all

the way to downtown Cleveland. These holes are all about seven miles long."

I had failed to change the scale. Pete was so mortified, he fired me as his mapmaker. I thought it was funnier than he did.

The Average Golfer

Do we design golf courses for the average golfer? Who is this man or woman? According to statistics, the man has a handicap of eighteen and drives the ball an average of 220 yards. The woman has a thirty-one handicap and drives the ball 130 yards. These golfers may belong to a private club or play at a daily fee course, and they play about twenty-five rounds a year. They love the game. Pete calls them "avid golfers."

Even on our most difficult courses designed for the PGA Tour play, we position tees with angles and yardages to create a challenging but manageable course for this gentleman and lady golfer. On PGA West, a course so difficult from the back tees that the PGA Tour players refused to play there, women golfers manage it beautifully and love the course.

However, the male avid golfer wants to try every difficult course that we have built, including PGA West,

Kiawah's Ocean Course, and Tournament Players Club. He will even travel to Scotland to play the great courses there. He will not go to the middle tees but will play from the tips and flail away, since he wants to play where the pros play or play the whole course. His drive may be many yards short of the professional's landing area, and he will probably never be able to post a score on any of these courses, but he played where the pros play, and that is all that matters to him. He will brag about how difficult the course was but will be excited about the one great shot he made on a particular hole. On his regular course, he will play the middle tees, wager with his buddies, and be able to turn in a score. We love these avid golfers because they love golf.

Restoring Courses

Our 1929 Model-T automobile has been restored to its original beauty, with only new brakes and shatterproof glass added for safety. It has a collapsible top and a rumble seat that can be converted into a trunk. It was a great automobile for the 1920s.

The golf courses built in that same era by such master architects as Donald Ross, Allister MacKenzie, and Seth Raynor were designed for the clubs, balls, and mowing

equipment of their time. They were great courses with bunkers designed to direct play with the expected length of shots in those days.

These courses have endured many changes. Most notable are the irrigation systems, maturing trees, new tees (both longer and shorter), and new speed grasses on the greens. Technologically improved mowers now cut the greens to extremely low levels, allowing the ball to roll at unbelievably fast speeds.

Much of the strategy of the original design has been lost as a result of the power-hitting equipment and the lively ball used by the modern-day player. Long hitters easily fly the old bunkers positioned to dictate the path of play.

Should these courses be restored to their original design or remodeled to keep the architect's intended strategy? Do we want courses of the 1920s to be like our Model-T Ford, restored to the original but unacceptable for today's highways?

When Donald Ross was alive, he was eager to replace his original sand greens at Pinehurst with the more modern Bermuda grass structures. I believe if he and other architects of the past were alive today, they would be adapting their courses to the modern golf equipment, not restoring them to outdated playing fields. We have already remodeled Crooked Stick, Long Cove, Harbour Town, and many of our other courses to adapt to today's standards.

Every time we add one of the new speed grasses to our greens, we must soften the contours, or the slopes will be too difficult to play. Just as Donald Ross did at Pinehurst, we remodel, not restore. We hope no one will ever restore our sand bunkers to their original, outdated positions or re-create our severely contoured greens.

The New Technology

There is a collision between fine, old golf courses and the modern-day player's golf equipment. I remember when Ping clubs were first introduced, and I found they were easier to hit. I remember that if I hit a shot on the toe or the heel, it was not quite as good as if I hit it on the sweet spot but almost as good. With my old clubs, if I missed the sweet spot, the result was always a poor shot.

This was the first innovation I noticed. Then the golf balls kept getting better. They not only went farther, but the ball began to correct itself in the air. If you hit a great big hook, you still got a great big hook. But if you hit a slight hook, the ball appeared to straighten out. All of a sudden the golf ball was helping players.

Metal woods were next. I kept thinking there would be an "end-all club," but they keep improving. The club heads of metal woods keep getting bigger and driving the ball farther. The innovations keep coming, with no end in sight. The floodgates have been opened, and they will be hard to close.

The new technology is providing equipment that is overwhelming golf courses. Lengthening the yardage is not the answer. I do not think Augusta National did golf any favors by lengthening their course. The Masters golf tournament is an invitational, and they could have said, "If you want to play here, you will all use the same type of restricted ball." Then anyone playing would be competing on a course that was the same as the one Bobby Jones, Gene Sarazen, and Jack Nicklaus played.

All lengthening courses does is favor the longer hitters. The governing organizations are always saying they want to protect the integrity of the game and par. The definition of par in the USGA rulebook is the number of strokes it takes to reach the green plus two putting strokes. The long hitters can reach par fives in two, making them essentially par fours. On many courses, the long hitters can also drive one or two of the short par fours, making them play like par threes. Before these long-hitting players tee off, they are theoretically at least four or five under par.

These days, people in the gallery cannot even see the golf ball land when John Daly or Tiger Woods launches one of his booming drives. They still ooh and aah, but many times they have no idea whether the ball is in the fairway or in a hazard.

Improved technology can destroy the game of golf. I compare golf manufacturers to automobile manufacturers who build cars that can race down the freeway at more than one hundred miles per hour. In Europe there are few speed limits, so drivers can drive as fast as they want, but in the United States we have speed limits—fifty-five on many roads.

We have cars that can go a lot faster, but we restrict them by providing speed limits. This is what should happen with golf. We need to put some speed limits on golf balls and golf equipment.

Already there is a combination of a golf ball and driver that can launch a ball four hundred yards. What will this do to great old golf courses that have limited space? Governing organizations need the authority to say enough is enough before it is too late.

Criticism

There are more than one hundred Pete and Alice Dye golf courses scattered around the United States, the Dominican Republic, Japan, and Switzerland. Golfers of all ages and skill levels play them every day.

They may blast us when they are in trouble, but hopefully they will hit that one great shot they will remember and brag about.

When someone criticizes one of our golf holes, Pete handles it well. He just smiles and says, "Well, they must have liked the other seventeen."

Responsibility

Every time a woman is empowered to succeed, that success is likely to reproduce itself in the lives of other women.
—Gay Chuba Berry

When you have an opportunity to be a leader or assist a cause and you have the capability, there is a responsibility to act.

One of my biggest disappointments occurred when a woman assistant golf course superintendent did not accept the position of head superintendent at a major golf club. She was an extremely hard worker and possessed all the qualifications to step up. Women had been denied head positions at major golf clubs, and she could have paved the way for future women superintendents. This club had hosted major championships and would do so in the future. I encouraged her because I saw this as an opportunity for a real breakthrough. She declined the position for several reasons, none of which I considered compelling. She missed the chance to help other women in her profession. I was very disappointed, since I feel that if you have the talent and ability, the responsibility is there to act.

Doing things you do not want to do is a difficult part of life. After I became known for championing forward tees for women and other architectural efforts to improve courses for them, I was asked to speak publicly about those concepts. I was not a speaker, so it was very difficult for me. As a science major, I never had to give speeches in college. I never had speech training, and I was not comfortable speaking in front of an audience. I would write the speech on little cards and then basically read it. Pete would tell me, "You sound so stiff and stilted." That was easy for him to say, since he can speak easily about any subject in the world, including the history of the first swing Mary Queen of Scots made. He does not need a note card or anything. I am absolutely helpless in that situation, so I prepare, practice, change the speech, practice, change it again, and practice some more, hoping each speech will be the last one I ever have to give. Why do I do it? It is a responsibility.

When I was asked to become a future president of the American Society of Golf Course Architects, I knew it would be a four-year process. First I would be secretary, then treasurer the second year, vice president the third year, and in the final year, president of an all-male—except me—organization. I was very hesitant to take on that responsibility, wondering if I would look foolish and subject the organization to ridicule. My reason for accepting the responsibility and possible fallout was not only to try to be a good leader for the society, but by being more visible, hopefully to open the door for other women to consider a career in golf course architecture and be accepted into the society.

Paul Fullmer, the executive director of the society, has called me a trailblazer for the group, and indeed, more women have become eligible and been welcomed into the American Society of Golf Course Architects.

PGA Lawsuit

In 1977 an attorney friend of mine called me for some assistance with a lawsuit. His client was a woman who had retired from the army and was the head professional at a nine-hole golf facility in Atlanta, Georgia.

In order for her golf shop assistants to gain credit toward becoming PGA members, they were required to work under a professional who was a member of the PGA. At that time, there were no women members of the PGA, but she applied and passed the preliminary tests.

The toughest obstacle was the Playing Ability Test. It required her to shoot an average of 75 from the men's tees on a course with a distance of approximately 6,500 yards.

This was impossible for her and almost any woman at the time. My lawyer friend asked for my assistance in determining the distances that would allow a woman to play well enough to qualify. I researched the yardage of the Women's Western Open, the USGA Women's Open, and the tournaments on the LPGA Tour and gave a deposition detailing the yardages that the best women professionals and amateurs were playing in tournaments.

I knew the PGA was being unfair, and I wanted to help. The case went to court in 1978, and we won the lawsuit that made the PGA reduce their Playing Ability Test yardages for women and subsequently admit the first woman into the PGA.

Shortly after the lawsuit, Pete ran into Mark Cox, president of the PGA of America, at the Atlanta airport. He told Pete he was really angry with me for being involved in the lawsuit that helped women gain entry into the PGA. He felt it was a men's organization, and it should stay that way. He accosted Pete, saying, "What is your wife doing suing the PGA?"

Pete was aghast. He told Mark that it could not be his wife doing such a thing, as we were just starting out in the golf course architecture business and we certainly would not want to offend the PGA. Pete said it must be someone else named Alice Dye—positively not his wife.

When Pete arrived home that evening, he told me about Mark Cox's mistake. I told him it was not a mistake—I *was* the one helping to sue the PGA. He confronted me, saying, "How could you? Why would you do such a thing?" I said, "BECAUSE THEY WERE WRONG!"

Today the PGA is proud to have almost 800 women members and is actively seeking more.

She Simmers

Economically, golf needs women. Courses have become so expensive to maintain that they cannot afford to be empty during weekdays. Welcome, ladies, we need you. Come take lessons, pay green fees, ride carts, and eat something. Buy some clubs, bags, balls, socks, and golf outfits. But remember, until things change, you are not welcome weekend mornings, so stay home and cook.

When I was a child, the Indianapolis Athletic Club, located downtown on prestigious Meridian Street, was a combination hotel, dining facility, and ballroom in addition to the men's gymnasium. Most northern large cities had these establishments to accommodate men's winter exercise. The club had two entrances—one at the front of the building for men and one on the side for women. Even if my mother and father were attending a party together, she had to enter using the side door. Unbelievably, some clubs in certain cities still have this rule. What are they thinking? Tradition should not include discrimination.

The Old Days

One makes many friends while playing in golf tournaments. Although some twenty years younger than I, Debbie Raso was a special friend and a great traveling companion. She was about twenty-one years old when we first met at the Florida State Championship. Debbie was headed for a career on the LPGA Tour until she injured her back horsing around in a swimming pool.

While traveling together, Debbie would ask me questions about the past. She was not sure if I started golf with the gutta-percha ball—wooden shafts, long dress, and bonnet. Debbie, I did start with hickory shafts, but I wore short shorts.

I told her my childhood home had electric lights and indoor plumbing, but our farm cabin had an outhouse. Our home washing machine was in the basement and had a wringer on top. Clothes were hauled outdoors to line-dry or strung around the basement.

We had heat from a coal furnace but no air conditioning. During hot days, Mother would draw the living room draperies and set a fan to blow over a washtub filled with a block of ice.

We read books, listened to the radio, and played records on a Victrola. We did not own a television while I was growing up. Our first television was a Muntz, given to Pete and me in 1952 when our son Perry was born.

The icebox held a block of ice, but electric refrigerators were coming.

The milkman brought milk everyday. The cream was on top of the milk, under the bottle cap.

A man on a bicycle rode by and sharpened all the knives and scissors.

Cars were bigger and faster. There were no freeways, but there wasn't much traffic outside the city. I drove my college Buick V8 convertible 105 miles per hour before it shook.

My first trip on an airplane was an overnight flight from Indianapolis to Tucson, Arizona. The flight attendant made up a double-decker berth, just as they do on trains.

Golf course fairways were bluegrass, cut about an inch high. The rough was weedy, with dandelions and buckhorn. There were a few ladies' tees but lots of roll everywhere.

Golf bags were small—caddies carried them and learned the game.

Many changes have been great. I just wish the man on the bicycle would come by and sharpen my scissors and that my golf shots would roll farther again.

Perfect Age

What age would you be if you didn't know how old you was?
—Satchel Paige

I was playing my favorite non-Dye course, Pinehurst Number 2, in a foursome of fellow senior ladies. One player in the group remarked how she would like to go back in age, still knowing what she knows now. We all agreed and then started discussing what age we would like to revisit. How about high school? There was a chorus of no's, since the teenage years are so difficult.

When we suggested our college days, it brought more no's; we all agreed that it was a difficult time, studying, dating, and choosing a career or marriage. We moved on to our middle twenties, with crying babies, sleepless nights, diapers, and baby-sitters. No one wanted to go through that again. Even knowing what we do now, none of us wanted to try our thirties again as parents of volatile, moody teenagers with new drivers' licenses. Finally, we got to age forty-five before any one of us wanted to go back. Considering we were only in our early fifties, we did not have to go back very far. We decided we were very lucky with our lives.

Skirting Disaster

In the 1940s, while I was playing golf as a teenager, shorts were acceptable for youngsters, but female players eighteen years and older wore skirts and even dresses. Both Babe Zaharias and Louise Suggs designed and sold a line of dresses with buttons down the front, slit sleeves, a gusset in the back, and a flowing skirt. The materials were mostly a cotton print with elastic in the gusset behind the shoulders. Players like Peggy Kirk (Bell), Dot Kielty, Patty Berg, and Polly Riley all wore straight belted skirts that hung below the knee. Shoes were white, brown, or a brown saddle.

Many clubs would not allow women to play in shorts or slacks. As late as 1972, at the USGA Women's Open at the Winged Foot Golf Club, the entry form did not advise us that the club would allow only skirts. Many of the players, both professional and amateur, had to borrow one. My skirt was a disaster—too big, too long, and too many pleats in the breeze. The press remarked we looked like a bunch of unplayable lies.

When I visited Australia in the 1980s, I packed navy slacks, white shirts, and a red sweater, thinking these would be acceptable everywhere. Times had advanced only a little there, as I could play golf in slacks but not eat lunch in the dining room wearing them.

In 1994, when Carol Semple Thompson was invited to

serve on the Executive Committee of the USGA, she had to attend a welcoming dinner. Since it was not an occasion to wear the committee blue blazer, she had to find an appropriate dinner outfit. With help from her mother, Phyllis Semple, and her friends, she found a perfect cream-colored jacket-and-pants evening suit. She looked great, and it was her style. Arriving in San Francisco for the dinner, she found out at the last minute that women could not enter the dining room in pants—no matter how flowing and elegant. She had quite a scramble finding a suitable long skirt to comply with the ridiculous, antiquated rule still in effect at many establishments.

Dress Code

Being the first woman member of any organization requires many decisions about the dress code. When I was accepted into the American Society of Golf Course Architects, their red Donald Ross plaid material was mailed to my home. I could use the yardage to construct any kind of apparel—coat, cape, skirt, vest, sash—as it came with no instructions. There was enough material for an entire outfit. Many fashionable ideas crossed my mind, but I elected to have a classic woman's single-breasted jacket tailored.

The first occasion to wear my jacket was at the Donald Ross dinner in Palm Springs, California, honoring Dinah Shore. With my jacket, I wore a white blouse, a wide navy bow tie, and dark silk slacks. It was very classic but still feminine.

When our car arrived at the entrance of the restaurant, there was a group of the gentlemen society members standing outside. When I got out of the car, it was their first chance to check out how I would dress. They approved. They clapped. I had been accepted.

When, at Jim Awtrey's invitation, I agreed to serve on the Board of Directors of the PGA, I dressed carefully for the first meeting. I wore black slacks, a white shirt, and a cashmere cardigan sweater. As I was standing in front of the room with the other new board members to be sworn in, I looked out at the hundreds of delegates and realized I was the only person in the room not wearing a jacket. I owned a blue Women's Western jacket, a navy USGA jacket, the Donald Ross plaid jacket, a Harbour Town plaid jacket, a red Mad Anthony's jacket, a Captain of the World Team jacket, and a Curtis Cup jacket. I now needed business-type jackets for meetings and PGA jackets for their special events. However, it was easier for me to buy new jackets than it was for the PGA to deal with their first female board member.

All of the PGA correspondence asked me to wear "a jacket and tie" and bring my "wife." The company that made the official rings for the board members made them only in men's designs and sizes. A company that tailors men's clothing exclusively made the required special events outfits, and mine were totally unrelated to my body. Pant zippers were on the wrong side, and the men's PGA emblem shirts were classy but too tight in the chest, with shirttails that never ended.

Pete's gift at one Champion's Dinner was a Tiffany sterling silver beaded necklace and bracelet set. My gift was an elegant cigar humidor.

Eventually, everyone adjusted. Now all PGA correspondence says, "business attire" and "bring your spouse." For the 2001 Ryder Cup, my emblem shirts were women's. My term as a board member has been completed, but my closet is full of jackets.

Equal Opportunities

When a woman steps up to the first tee, she loses her status as a female, becomes a golf player, and assumes all the rights and responsibilities of a player. There are skilled or struggling women players, just as there are skilled or struggling men players. Every player has an obligation to the pace of play. A foursome of gentlemen players with open holes ahead should allow a waiting foursome of women players to play through. This does not happen often.

One day at the Crooked Stick Golf Club, professional Jim Ferriell realized that a foursome with guests trying to post a good score would be deliberate with their play. When he saw my foursome of low-handicap women tee off, he knew we would soon catch them. We did, but when we arrived at the par-three sixth tee, Jim had come from the golf shop and asked the gentlemen on the green to allow us to play through. We accepted, all hit the green, putted, and quickly walked off to the next tee, but not so quickly that we failed to hear one man's comment, "Well, that's a first."

Two-Tee System for Women

Before 1950 only golf course tees and greens were watered. Fairways were firm, and balls would roll great distances.

When the watering systems began to drench fairways, the usual 6,200 yards for women began to play much longer. Believing women should have a course that was manageable for them and have the same option as men to have a choice of teeing grounds of different yardages, I created a chart and videotape diagramming positions and lengths of a two-tee system for women.

When I presented the video to a joint meeting of the USGA men's and women's handicap committees, the suggested short yardage of 4,800 to 5,200 yards was met with derogatory comments of "Mickey Mouse golf" and "not a whole course" by the women who were mostly accomplished players. The gentlemen present who had to play with their less skilled wives were silent. Later, the male staff of the USGA offered to help me by endorsing forward yardages, but I was afraid that clubs would rush out and indiscernibly put in little forward tees without considering the playability of the hole.

More sympathetic to my ideas, the members of the American Society of Golf Course Architects began incorporating multiple tees with shorter yardages for the forward positions, so my suggested yardages have slowly evolved, but a two-tee system has not been accepted. There is more of a spread of strength between women players than between men players, but men have at least two and as many as four tees. Women play from the same tee and refuse to budge!

And the Walls Will Come Tumbling Down

The walls of men-only clubs, men's grills, and membership in only a man's name are being attacked. It may not be the women's organizations that will create change but the fathers and grandfathers of girls who realize their female child is being discriminated against.

A girl raised at a country club, with her social life revolving around her friends there, cannot become a member, but her brother can. A father who watched his daughter and her friends swim, play tennis, golf, and attend the club social events is not going to stand for such discrimination. As a member of his club, it will be this father who crumbles the wall. It was the father of a daughter who was discriminated against when she attempted to be a judge in Texas who opened the door for me to become the first woman member of the American Society of Golf Course Architects.

Fathers today watching their daughters play in high school soccer, basketball, hockey, or golf competitions need to be grateful to their own fathers, who braved criticism and the courts to ensure that the old discriminatory rules of the High School Athletic Associations were challenged so girls could participate. Then in 1972 Title IX came to college-level athletics. The rules governing Title IX are complicated and constantly being rewritten and enforced by the Supreme Court, but the concept of gender equality is attainable.

Annika's Everest

If a mountain is there, it beckons mankind to climb it. The PGA Tour is like a mountain for Annika Sorenstam—it is there, and she wants to attempt to play on it.

For mountain climbers, whether they make the summit or not, it is the attempt that challenges them. So it is with Annika. She wants to challenge herself to compete against the mountain of the PGA Tour. It should not matter how she finishes. Just because it is there, she must try. She will not be the last.

Dinner with the President

No weather is too blustery for former president George H. Bush to play a round of golf. He came to Herb Kohler's magnificent Whistling Straits Golf Course in 1991 to play the opening round of the course

Pete had just constructed. Herb Kohler envisioned the Whistling Straits course after golf trips to Ireland and Scotland. He found a strip of bluff along the shores of Lake Michigan and told Pete he wanted him to build a course like Ballybunion. The lake was washing away the shoreline, and eventually the bluff would tumble down, so Pete was able to get a permit to start at the shoreline and slope back the bluff. Pete, with his vivid imagination, molded the soil of the bluff into high mounds and covered them with sand, bringing Ireland's sand dunes to the United States.

The president, refusing Herb Kohler's offer of a wager for more than a dollar Nassau, bundled up and braved the damp, cold, windy weather. After the round, Pete and I were invited to join the president and Natalie and Herb Kohler for dinner at eight o'clock.

At six-thirty I was showered and relaxing in my room at the luxurious American Club when Pete burst in and said the president wanted to eat earlier, and everyone was waiting for us. I grabbed my dress and slipped it over my head, scrambling to get dressed. Rushing to the elegant, formal dining room, I saw an empty chair next to the president, where I had been honored to sit. Sliding in with vague apologies, Pete and I sat down, and the waiters began serving. My sleeves felt awkward, and the dress was creeping up the front of my neck. As each course progressed, the dress continued upward until it was about to strangle me. If the president noticed this new fashion, he discreetly did not comment. By dessert, I realized I had the dress on backward.

Oak Tree Almost Beats Seminole

Pete and I built the Oak Tree Golf Club in Edmond, Oklahoma, site of the 1988 PGA Championship, for Landmark Company and our good friends Ernie Vossler and Joe Walser. After their course opened, Joe visited Florida, and Pete invited him to play at the Seminole Golf Club, the gem designed by Donald Ross in 1928.

Before playing, Pete and Joe selected from the lunch buffet. Joe commented that he enjoyed the fine food, but the menu at Oak Tree had more variety: Mexican beans, Doritos, barbeque, and such. They then headed to the locker room, and while they were removing their jackets and changing into golf shoes, Joe noted that the cathedral locker room was magnificent, but Oak Tree's facility offered more amenities, including warmed towel racks.

Pete and Joe proceeded to play the first nine holes and then stopped at the drink stand. Joe said it was nice, but the stand at Oak Tree was more elaborate. After playing the final nine holes, Joe voiced his opinion that while

Seminole was a fine golf course, Pete had built him a better one at Oak Tree. Then Joe looked over at the practice tee. There was Ben Hogan all alone, hitting practice balls. Joe studied the scene, looked at Pete, grinned, and said, "Well, I guess having Ben Hogan on the practice tee *does* make a difference."

Foot in Mouth

Age is in the eye of the beholder, but George Peper, former editor of *Golf Magazine* and a fine author, really embarrassed himself when he misjudged mine.

George and David Fay, executive director of the USGA, joined us for dinner at the Casa de Campo resort in the Dominican Republic. We dined on a patio overlooking the Caribbean Sea. I sat at one end of the table, with George and David on either side of me. An afternoon at the beauty shop, the candlelight, and the flower-filled table made me feel especially youthful.

The talk turned to golf, and George asked, "Alice, I have to ask you, with all your playing accomplishments, with all the tournaments you have won, all the low rounds you have posted over your long and glittering career, have you ever achieved the goal that every golfer wants most?" I thanked George for his kind comments and said, "What's that?" He shifted in his chair as the moon reflected off the water and said, "Have you ever shot your age?" With complete devastation, I looked squarely at George and said, "George, I'm *only* fifty-seven." In a future edition of *Golf*, George wrote the following:

Oh, my God. How do I spell mortified? What could I possibly say to clean up after myself? As David Fay masked his giddy delight behind a napkin, my mind reeled with a list of exculpatory repartees: I know that, I just thought you were a better player; I meant shoot your age for 15 holes, you silly goose; No, no you misheard me, I said "Have you ever shed your AIDS?" All were rejected in favor of a simple "Gee, I'm sorry." Not surprisingly, Alice handled it more gracefully than I did, and by the time I'd pried my size 11 [shoe] out of my mouth, the group had moved on to other subjects, except for Fay, who continued to wipe tears of hilarity from his eyes.

Whenever I saw him, I would ask, "George, shot your age yet?" Pete got him back too. When they were playing together at one of our new golf courses, I approached in a golf cart. Pete said, "Hey, George, here comes that old bag of a wife of mine." Finally, thirteen years later in

1997, a great round allowed me to write George a letter. It read: "George, I've finally done the deed. I shot my age—a 70 at Gulfstream Golf Club. Wanted you to be the first to know. Fondly, Alice."

Ageless

Peggy Kirk Bell, an outstanding teaching golf professional, is a great role model for those who complain about age. When she was seventy-eight, a club in India asked her to travel there and teach for a week. She tried to beg off, saying she thought they needed someone younger. They told her they were looking for a teacher that was "older with wisdom." She finally agreed to go and was a huge success. Peggy is now in her eighties, and she is the most sought-after teacher at her beloved Pine Needles Club in Southern Pines, North Carolina.

At a municipal course in Hollywood, Florida, one morning, I noticed a lady finishing her ninth hole while I was teeing off from the first hole at nine-thirty. I asked someone who she was, and they said she was ninety-nine years old and played golf every morning. The next day

I saw her in the clubhouse. I asked why she played so early. She replied, "I have to catch the bus at eleven-thirty so I can make my line-dancing class."

My friend Shannon told me this story. She had played golf for many years and upon turning fifty, entered her first USGA Women's Senior tournament. After the final practice round, Shannon joined the other contestants at the formal pretournament dinner. She was seated at a table of eight between two contestants she did not know. Being a friendly sort, she attempted to make conversation in spite of the din the waiters made clanking their trays. To the lady on the right, Shannon asked, "Is that a Diana Freese dress you are wearing?" The lady smiled and said, "It *is* chilly in here, isn't it?" Shannon nodded.

Moments later, she decided to try again and turned to the lady on her left, saying, "Isn't this a delicious dinner?" The lady replied, "Thank you. I bought it at Saks." Welcome to the seniors, Shannon!

Judy Bell

Sitting in his library with Harton "Bud" Semple, past president of the USGA and that year head of the Nominating Committee for the USGA, I broached the subject of selecting a woman for the all-male Executive Committee of the USGA. I had in mind Judy Bell, who had just completed her last term as head of the USGA Women's Committee. Judy had been a top ranked amateur, a member and captain of the Curtis Cup Team, and captain of the World Golf Team, and was loved by fellow committee members and her team players. She had several successful clothing shops, a deli, and other diversified businesses, and was dedicated to golf.

Women admired Judy and, more importantly, so did men. She could work well with both. It was the perfect opportunity for the USGA to put a woman on their Executive Committee before someone made an issue of the organization's all-male leadership.

Bud Semple was an attorney and a very fair-minded gentleman. He was also the father of a son and four daughters. Bud nominated Judy Bell to be the first woman on the USGA Executive Committee. He took a great deal of criticism from his compatriots, but Judy served so well she went on to be elected president of the USGA. Bud Semple did not live to see it, but his own daughter Carol would follow Judy as the second woman member of the USGA Executive Committee.

Soap Friends

Years ago I had a close friend who was dying of cancer. She was bedridden and could hardly talk, but we could watch television together. We shared the initial episode of the soap opera, *The Young and the Restless.*

I have lost my dear friend but have continued to watch *The Young and the Restless* since her death. The characters on the soap are my friends, and when I travel, they follow me to hotel rooms wherever I am—California, Wisconsin, New York, and even the Dominican Republic. Whenever I am in my own home and cannot watch the show, I tape it. The lead male character, Victor Newman (aka Eric Braeden), has married practically every woman who has ever been on the show. In an episode one Friday, he was in a horrendous, fiery automobile crash. The following Sunday I was a spectator at the Indianapolis 500 race when "Victor" sat down next to me. I gasped, "Are you all right?" He laughed while saying, "Tune in Monday."

Great People in a Great Game

After being eliminated from match play in the Women's North and South Tournament played at Pinehurst Number 2, I was walking with former USGA president and part owner Richard Tuffs and spectating the quarterfinal matches. We stood beside the fourteenth green and watched the eight fine players come through. I commented on their gracious behavior.

Responding, Mr. Tuffs said, "Alice, there are no bad people in golf. The game drives them out. In golf, players are their own referee and scorekeeper. You are responsible for your behavior, and if you do not act right and follow the rules, no one will play with you, and soon you drop out."

I thought about all the fine people I know in golf, and I knew Mr. Tuffs was right. When most amateurs are asked what they like best about golf, the answer is almost always, "The friends I have made."

Continuing our conversation, Mr. Tuffs told me the history of the greens at Pinehurst 2. He said that the reason the greens had the raised-angel-cake effect was that for years they were top-dressed with sand to just the edge of the putting surface. The fringes were not top-dressed, so over the years the putting surface was raised almost twelve inches, creating a drop-off to the fringe.

At that time, the greens were not crowned but had an average of 6,000 square feet of putting surface on top, with some swales for drainage. Since then, with each of the many grass changes, the edges have gradually been lost, creating smaller actual putting surfaces and a crowned effect. What would Pinehurst architect Donald Ross say about these new turtle-backed greens on his great golf course? I do not think he would like them.

EPILOGUE

Friends reading Pete's book, *Bury Me in a Pot Bunker,* tell me it is our love story. I agree.

Pete has been the cheerleader for this book and for me ever since we met at Rollins College. The first spring of our marriage, he brought me a new shag bag of balls to motivate me to practice and play. He always helped me prepare for tournaments and watched whenever he could. He even wheeled our two-year-old son Perry around the golf course in a rickety baby stroller to watch me win the Indiana State Championship.

Pete has always been a great father to our sons. He attended every scheduled event when he was not traveling. He encouraged them in their careers and helped when requested.

Pete asked me to be his partner in the golf course design and building adventure. He encouraged me to work on the USGA and Women's Western Committees, to join the American Society of Golf Course Architects, and to accept the invitation from the PGA of America to their Board of Directors. He has always listened to my ideas and suggestions about golf course design.

Best of all, Pete has always been himself—the same man with his carefree antics and fun-loving attitude. It's been a Fourth of July kind of life together.

Beneath all of this is a man with strong values, dedicated to his family and his work. He demands the best of himself and of those who work with him. He wanted me to write this book, so I did it for him.

—Alice Dye

ACKNOWLEDGMENTS

The authors wish to thank the following people for their assistance with *From Birdies to Bunkers:*

Pete Dye
Shannon Meeks
Robin Weiss Donnelley
Carol Semple Thompson
Wayne Timberman Jr.
Chris Shaw
Paul Fullmer

Diane Darsch
Carolyn Lautner
Perry O'Neal
Natalie Kohler
Rudy Crabtree
Jerry Bales
Jim Awtrey

Special thanks go to literary agent Carolyn Carney and to Megan Newman and Matthew Benjamin at Harper-Collins for believing in the book.

INDEX

Page numbers in *italics* refer to illustrations.

ABOUT THE AUTHORS

Alice Dye is a championship golfer and golf course architect who, along with husband, Pete, has created many Top 100 golf courses in America. Alice was the first woman president of the American Society of Golf Course Architects and the first woman member of the PGA of America Board of Directors. She and Pete reside in Carmel, Indiana, and Delray Beach, Florida. Pete is the author of *Bury Me in a Pot Bunker*, with Mark Shaw.

Mark Shaw, a longtime friend of Alice and Pete Dye, is a lawyer turned author, with twelve published books. They include *Bury Me in a Pot Bunker*, with Pete Dye, *Jack Nicklaus: Golf's Greatest Champion*, *Forever Flying*, *Larry Legend*, *Book Report*, *The Perfect Yankee*, *Miscarriage of Justice*, and *Testament to Courage*.